The OFFICIAL 9mm Makarov Pistol Manual

Originally Issued by
the Ministry of Defense of the U.S.S.R.

Translated by James F. Gebhardt
Edited by Scott Blazey
Technical Editing by Roger L. Heinen

Desert Publications
El Dorado, AR 71731-1751

The Official 9mm Makarov Pistol Manual

Published by Desert Publications
215 S. Washington
El Dorado, AR 71730
info@deltapress.com

10 9 8 7 6 5 4 3 2
ISBN: 0-87947-146-8
Printed in U. S. A.

Desert Publication is a division of
The DELTA GROUP, Ltd.
Direct all inquiries & orders to the above address.

This manual was originally published in the Soviet Union under the title *Nastavleniye po strelkovomu delu 9-mm pistolet Makarova,* (third edition under the supervision of Lieutenant Colonel N. N. Plamitsin, edited by I. K. Vil'chinskiy, technical editor G. F. Sokolov, proofreader G. M. Ugarov.

Neither the author nor the publisher assumes any responsibility for the use or misuse of the information contained in this book. This material was compiled for educational and entertainment purposes and one should not construe that any other purpose is suggested.

ABOUT THE BOOK

Since 1951, the 9mm Makarov Pistol has been the standard sidearm of the armed forces of the Soviet Union (and now of the nations which once comprised the U.S.S.R.) It is a well-designed and well-built weapon with a reputation for reliability when cared for and used properly. The Manual of Instructions for Use and Maintenance of the 9mm Makarov Pistol (Third Edition), published in 1957 by the U.S.S.R. Ministry of Defense was intended for distribution and use by military and paramilitary organizations equipped with the Makarov pistol. Its equivalent in the U.S. Army would be a technical manual in the -10 series, that is, an operator/user manual.

This excellent and detailed manual is now available, in English, for the many thousands of firearms enthusiasts who have acquired the 9mm Makarov pistol made in the former Soviet Union, or one of the former Soviet bloc countries. The Russian-to-English translation was painstakingly crafted by James Gebhardt, a recognized expert in Soviet military history and an experienced translator of Russian documents.

The information contained in these pages will be of enormous benefit and interest as a historical reference to owners and users of 9mm Makarov Pistols.

While the pistol is commonly referred to as the 9mm Makarov, owners and users should note that the original pistols were chambered for the 9mm x 18mm cartridge. This is different than the 9mm Parabellum or 9mm Luger cartridge common in many autoloading pistols. Some newly manufactured Makarov pistols are chambered for the .380 ACP cartridge. The use and maintenance of the Makarov pistol as described in this manual is essentially the same, regardless of the caliber or country of manufacture.

Following the translation of the Makarov manual is a special section on firearms safety. Owners and users of the Makarov pistol are strongly encouraged to study this section and practice safe handling of firearms and ammunition at all times.

ABOUT THE DESIGNER

Nikolay Fedorovich Makarov was born in 1914 in Sasevo, a small town in Russia about 200 miles southeast of Moscow. His father was a machinist for the railroad. At age 15, in 1929, Makarov entered an apprentice training school for metal workers in Ryazan, and worked in a steam locomotive repair facility through 1935. From 1936 to 1941, he was a student at the Tula Mechanical Institute. Makarov worked as a shift foreman, shop foreman, and head designer in a Soviet defense plant that manufactured the Shpagin 7.62mm submachinegun (PPSh-41 and variants) during the Great Patriotic War. From 1945 until his retirement in 1974, Makarov worked at a weapons design bureau. Over the span of his career, Makarov received many awards and decorations in recognition of his numerous inventions and designs in the field of Soviet military small arms: Hero of Socialist Labor, two awards of the State Prize of the U.S.S.R., the S.I. Mosin Prize, two Orders of Lenin, and the Order of the Red Banner of Labor.

Source: D.N. Bolotin, Sovetskoye strelkovoye oruzhiye [Soviet Infantry Weapons] 2d Edition, Moscow: Voyenizdat, 1986, pp 97-98.

ABOUT THE TRANSLATOR

James F. Gebhardt is a retired U.S. Army officer who served as an enlisted infantryman (1966-69), armor officer (1974-83), and Soviet foreign area officer (1984-91). He is the author of *Leavenworth Papers No. 17, The Petsamo-Kirkenes Operation: Soviet Breakthrough and Pursuit in the Arctic, October 1944,* (Ft. Leavenworth, KS: USACGSC, 1990), the first study in English of a little known Soviet offensive in the rugged terrain northwest of Murmansk, based primarily on Russian-language sources. While an analyst at the Soviet Army Studies Office, Fort Leavenworth, Gebhardt authored several articles on Soviet Army tactics and Soviet Army and Navy special operations forces. His latest work is Blood on the Shores: Soviet Naval Commandos in World War II (Annapolis: Naval Institute Press, 1993), an expanded translation of the combat memoir of Twice Hero of the Soviet Union Viktor Leonov, famed naval scout of the Northern and Pacific Fleets.

Gebhardt studied the Russian language at the University of Idaho at Moscow (BA, Political Science, 1974), the University of Washington at Seattle (MA, Soviet History, 1976), Defense Language Institute at Presidio of Monterey, California, (Diploma, 1984), and the U.S. Army Russian Institute at Garmisch, Federal Republic of Germany (Diploma, 1986). He has performed military duty in the Soviet Union, and has escorted numerous Soviet scientific, military, and diplomatic personnel on U.S. military installations in the United States.

Mr. Gebhardt currently works as a computer simulation specialist for a defense contractor at Fort Leavenworth, Kansas, and continues to translate Soviet and Russian military historical materials in his spare time.

NOTICE

Various federal, state, and local laws govern the transfer and transportation of firearms. If you do not know the applicable laws, consult a firearms dealer or a law enforcement official in your area prior to transferring or transporting any firearm.

If there is anything you do not understand regarding the use and operation of the Makarov Pistol or any firearm seek advice from someone qualified in the safe handling of firearms.

This instruction manual is intended only as an historical reference document. It was originally published in Russian by the Ministry of Defense of the Union of Soviet Socialist Republics Military Press in 1957 as an instruction manual for their military personnel on the use and maintenance of the 9mm Makarov Pistol. Although careful study of this translation could be potentially beneficial to anyone who owns or uses the Makarov Pistol, this translation is not intended to be an owner's or operator's safety and instruction manual for Makarov Pistols sold commercially as military surplus or as newly manufactured firearms.

Table of Contents

PART ONE
Construction of the Pistol, Its Handling, Care and Preservation

Table of Contents

Table of Contents

PART TWO
Methods and Conduct of Fire With the Pistol

PART ONE

CONSTRUCTION OF THE PISTOL, ITS HANDLING, CARE, AND PRESERVATION

Chapter 1

GENERAL INFORMATION

Nomenclature and combat capabilities of the pistol

1. The 9-mm Makarov pistol (figure 1) is a personal weapon for offense and defense, intended to defeat the enemy at short ranges.

This pistol fires 9-mm [9 x 18] pistol cartridges in single shots. The best results are achieved by firing the pistol at ranges up to 50 meters.

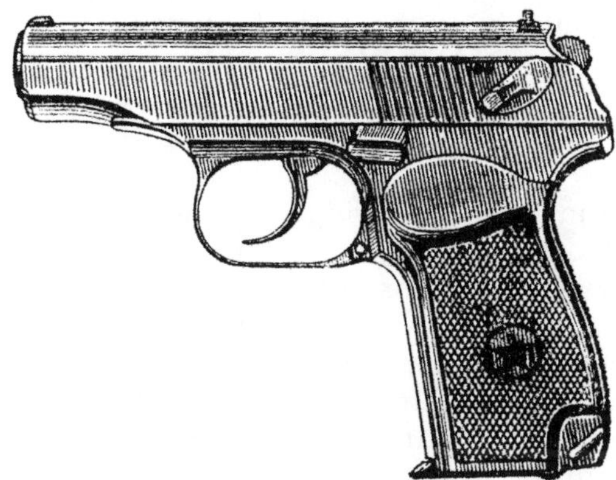

Figure 1. *General view of a 9-mm Makarov pistol.*

2. The combat rate of fire of this pistol is 30 rounds per minute.

Its muzzle velocity is 315 m/sec (1033 ft/sec).

The projectile remains lethal to a range of 350 meters.

The weight of the pistol with a loaded magazine is 810 grams (28 oz.).

Construction and function of the pistol's components

3. The pistol is simple in design and handling; it is small, light, convenient to carry, and always ready for action. The pistol is a self-loading weapon, because it reloads the subsequent round automatically, and fires one shot with each trigger pull. It is designed to use the recoil energy of the free slide. The self-cocking firing mechanism enables the firer to open fire quickly by squeezing the trigger, without first drawing back the hammer.

Safe handling of the pistol is ensured by a reliable safety latch. The pistol's thumb safety is located on the left side of the slide. In addition, the hammer automatically remains at a safe position under the action of the mainspring after releasing (decocking) the hammer.

Ammunition is fed into the pistol's action from an 8-round magazine.

4. The pistol consists of the following basic components and mechanisms (figure 2): receiver with barrel and trigger guard; slide with firing pin, extractor, and safety; recoil spring; trigger mechanism; one-piece handgrip with screw; slide stop; and magazine.

Each pistol comes with a cleaning rod, spare magazine, and holster.

5. The 9-mm pistol cartridge (figure 3) consists of the case, primer, powder charge, and projectile.

6. The pistol functions as follows:

When the trigger is squeezed, the hammer, freed from the sear, is driven by the mainspring to strike the firing pin, which drives forward against the primer of the cartridge. The combustion of the powder charge in the barrel generates gases that exert pressure in all directions. The pressure of these gases drives the projectile forward and through the barrel. At the

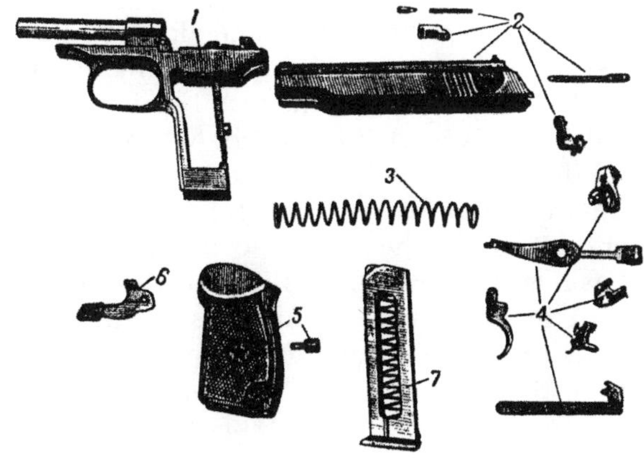

Figure 2. *Basic components and mechanisms of the pistol.*
1- receiver group
2 - slide group
3 - recoil spring
4 - trigger group and firing mechanism
5 - handgrips and screw
6 - slide stop
7 - magazine

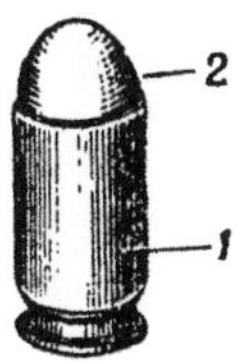

Figure 3. *General view of the 9-mm pistol cartridge.*
1 - casing
2 - projectile

same time, the pressure of the gases against the base of the cartridge case drives the slide rearward, causing the ejection of the case and the compression of the recoil spring. On striking the ejector, the case is ejected out of the weapon through the port in the slide.

While moving to its most rearward position, the slide rotates the hammer on its pin to the cocked position. When it reaches the limit of its rearward travel, the slide returns forward under the pressure of the recoil spring. During its forward movement, the slide picks up the next cartridge from the magazine and drives it forward and upward into the chamber. The barrel is locked by the free slide, and the pistol is again ready to fire.

To fire the subsequent shot, the firer simply releases the trigger and then squeezes it again. Thus, firing will be conducted until all the rounds are gone from the magazine. Upon expenditure of all the rounds in the magazine, the slide stop engages the slide and holds it in the rearward position.

Chapter 2

DISASSEMBLY, ASSEMBLY, CLEANING, AND LUBRICATING OF THE PISTOL

Disassembly and assembly

7. The pistol is disassembled to clean, lubricate, or inspect it, or to exchange or repair malfunctioning parts. Unnecessary disassembly is harmful, because it accelerates the wear of the pistol's components and mechanisms.

During disassembly and assembly of the pistol, it is necessary to observe the following rules:

— conduct disassembly and assembly on a table or bench. In the field, use a clean tarp;

— keep components in the order of disassembly, handle them carefully, and do not use excessive effort or sharp blows;

— during assembly, pay attention to the numbering of the parts, to avoid mixing them with parts from other pistols.

It is forbidden to exchange parts (safety, hammer, sear, trigger bar with cocking lever, firing pin) of different pistols, because this can lead to malfunctions and, in some cases, to unintentional discharge of the weapon.

8. Disassembly of the weapon can be either partial or total.

Partial disassembly is done to clean, lubricate, and inspect the pistol.

Full disassembly is done to replace malfunctioning parts, and in those cases when the pistol has fallen into water, been rained on, or dropped in dirt or snow, when changing to a different lubricant, or after prolonged firing.

9. Partial disassembly of the pistol is conducted in the following sequence:

a. Remove the magazine from the handgrip (figure 4). Hold the pistol by the handgrip in the right hand. With the thumb of the left hand, push the magazine release to the rear. Simultaneously, pull on the protruding part of the magazine floor with the index finger of the left hand, withdrawing the magazine from the handgrip.

Inspect to insure that there is no round in the chamber by taking the weapon off safe (press downward on the safety latch), draw the slide rearward with the left hand, and look into the chamber. Release the slide.

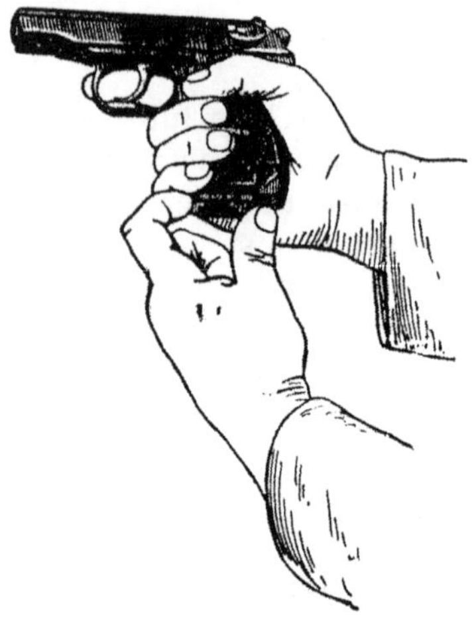

Figure 4. *Removal of the magazine from the handgrip.*

b. Separate the slide from the receiver. Hold the pistol by the handgrip in the right hand. With the left hand, pull downward on the forward end of the trigger guard (figure 5) and, pressing it to the left or right, let it rest against the frame where it will remain in this position. (It is preferable to press the forward end of the trigger guard to the left, so that during the subsequent disassembly it can be held in this position by the index finger of the right hand.)

With the left hand, pull the slide as far to the rear as it will go. Raise the rear end of the slide and let it go forward under the pressure of the recoil spring. Separate the slide from the receiver (figure 6) and return the forward portion of the trigger guard to its normal position.

c. Remove the recoil spring from the barrel. Hold the receiver by the handgrip in the right hand. With the left hand, draw the recoil spring forward and remove it from the barrel.

Figure 5. *Pulling away front portion of trigger guard.*

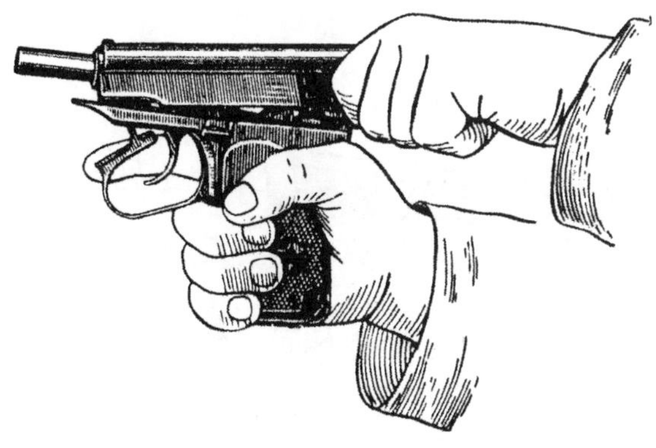

Figure 6. *Removal of slide from receiver.*

10. Assembly of the pistol after partial disassembly is conducted in the following sequence:

a. Place the recoil spring on the barrel. Hold the receiver by the handgrip in the right hand. With the left hand, place the recoil spring on the barrel, with the smallest coil of the spring going onto the barrel first.

b. Join the slide to the receiver. Hold the receiver by the handgrip in the right. With the left hand, pull downward on the forward end of the trigger guard and, pressing it to the left or right, let it rest against the frame where it will remain in this position. With the slide in the left hand, place the free end of the recoil spring in the slide channel (figure 7). Pull the slide to its most rearward position so that the muzzle end of the barrel protrudes through the slide channel (figure 8). Place the rear portion of the slide on the receiver so that the longitudinal guides of the slide engage the channels of the receiver and, pressing the slide onto the receiver, release it. The recoil spring will energetically return the slide to the forward position. [Editor's note: Slight pressure or manipulation of the slide may be necessary to facilitate forward seating.]

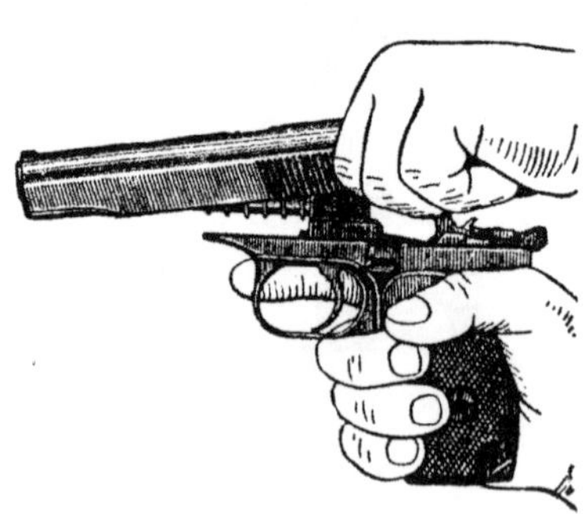

Figure 7. Placement of free end of recoil spring into slide channel.

Figure 8. Joining slide to receiver.

Engage the safety (rotate the lever upward).

c. Insert the magazine into the handgrip. Hold the pistol in the right hand. Using the thumb and index finger of the left hand, insert the magazine intc the handgrip through the lower opening of the handgrip frame (figure 9). Press on the magazine floor plate with the thumb so that the catch (lower end of the mainspring) engages the recess on the back wall of the magazine. There should be an audible "click" when this occurs.

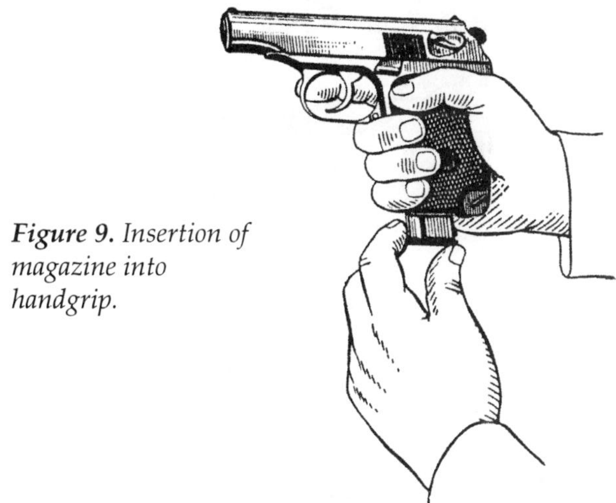

Figure 9. *Insertion of magazine into handgrip.*

11. Confirm the correct assembly of the pistol after partial disassembly. Disengage the safety (rotate the latch downward). Draw the slide to the rear and let it go. The slide, having gone a short distance forward under the action of the recoil spring, should be stopped in the rearward position by the slide stop. Press on the slide stop button. Under the action of the recoil spring, the slide should energetically return to the forward position, and the hammer should be cocked. Engage the safety (rotate the latch upward). The hammer should come forward off the cocked position.

12. Complete disassembly of the pistol is conducted in the following sequence:

a. Partially disassemble the pistol as previously instructed (paragraph 9).

b. Remove the sear and slide stop from the receiver. Hold the hammer spur with the thumb of the right hand. Press the trigger with the index finger to release the hammer smoothly from full cock.

With the cleaning rod or the magazine floor plate, remove the trigger spring sear from the edge of the slide stop (figure 10). With the index finger of the right hand, rotate the sear forward until the flat on the right pin aligns with the slot of the pin housing in the receiver. Then lift the sear and slide stop upward and separate them from the receiver (figure 11).

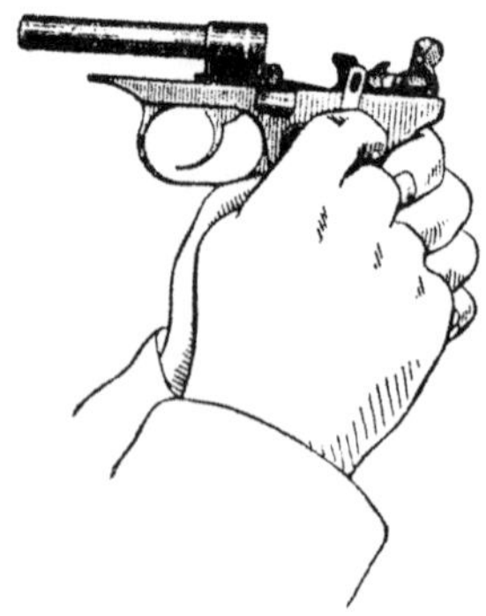

Figure 10. *Removal of trigger sear spring from ledge of slide stop.*

Figure 11. *Removal of sear and slide stop from receiver.*

c. **Remove pistol grip from handgrip frame and mainspring from receiver.** Remove the screw at the back of the handgrip with the screwdriver tip on the cleaning rod handle. With a little effort, pull the grip rearward and separate it from the handgrip frame (figure 12.)

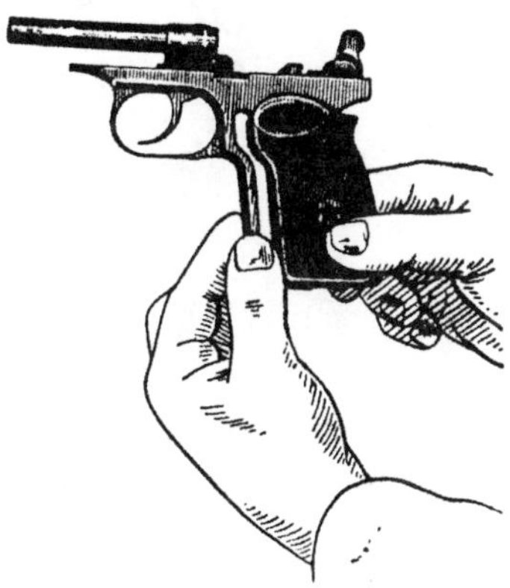

Figure 12. *Removal of handgrips from frame.*

Pull downward and separate the mainspring retainer from the receiver, and remove the mainspring from the locating lug on the handgrip frame.

Notes:

1. In combat conditions, if there is no screwdriver blade available, the screw can be backed out by using the slide lock.

2. In early production models, the mainspring is mounted without a retainer.

d. Remove hammer from receiver. Hold the receiver in the left hand and return the trigger to its most forward position. Using the thumb and index finger of the right hand, rotate the hammer forward until the flats on its pin align with the slots of its pin housing in the receiver. Then move the hammer toward the barrel and remove it (figure 13).

Figure 13. *Removal of hammer from receiver.*

e. Remove the trigger bar with cocking lever from the receiver. Hold the receiver in the left hand. With the right hand, lift up the back end of the trigger bar (figure 14) and remove the pin from the hole of the trigger.

f. Remove the trigger from the receiver. Hold the receiver in the right hand. With the left hand, pull down on the forward

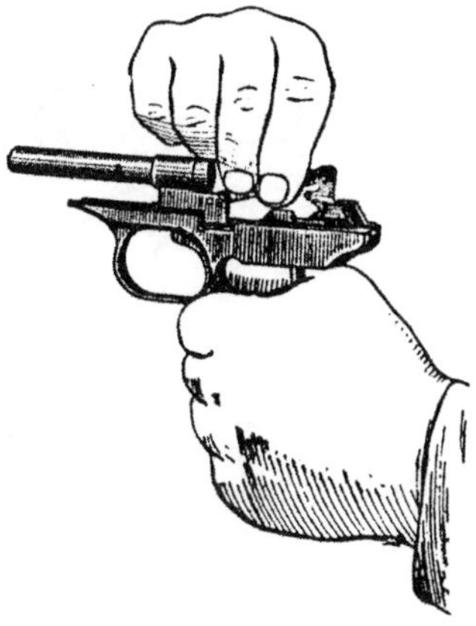

Figure 14. *Removal of trigger bar with cocking lever from receiver.*

end of the trigger guard, as was done during partial disassembly of the pistol (paragraph 9). Rotating the trigger forward, remove the pin from its seat in the receiver and separate the trigger from the receiver.

Reposition the forward end of the trigger guard to its seat.

g. Remove the safety and firing pin from the slide. Hold the slide in the left hand. Using the thumb of the right hand, rotate the safety upward. Then, with the index finger and thumb of the right hand, pull the safety lever outward from its seat and rotate it slightly to the rear to remove it from the slide (figure 15).

Dislodge the firing pin from the slide by lightly tapping the rear of the slide against the palm of the right hand.

h. Remove the extractor from the slide (figure 16). Hold the slide in the left hand. With the right hand, use a small drift to depress the plunger. Pry upward at the rear portion of the extractor and remove it from its seat in the slide, controlling the extractor with the thumb of the left hand to prevent it from flying out. Remove the plunger, with extractor, from its seat in the slide.

Note: The extractor is removed from the slide only when the pistol is being disassembled for cleaning after it has been in water or exposed to rain, and also when transitioning the pistol from summer lubricants to winter lubricants and vice versa.

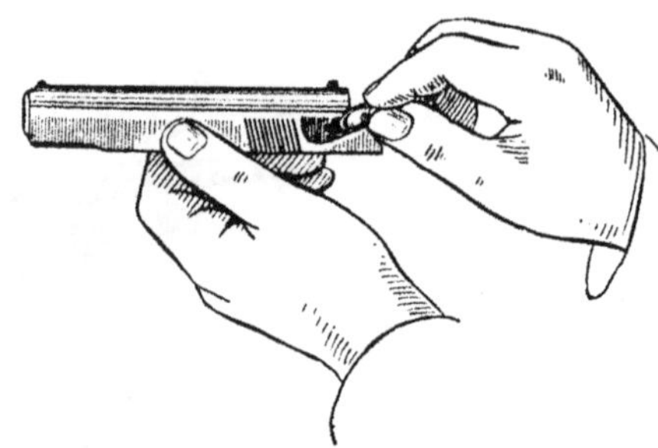

Figure 15. Removal of safety from slide.

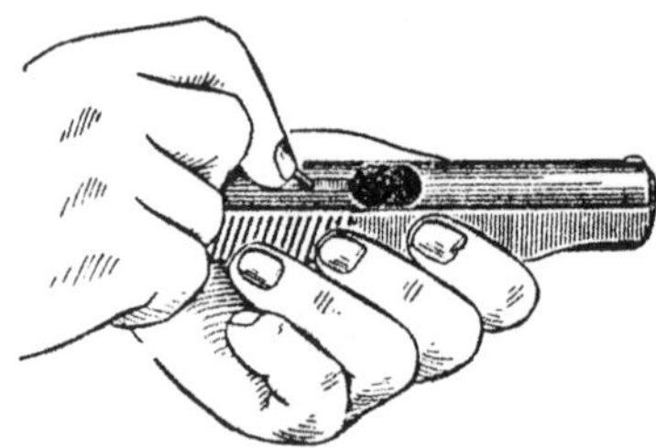

Figure 16. Removal of extractor from slide.

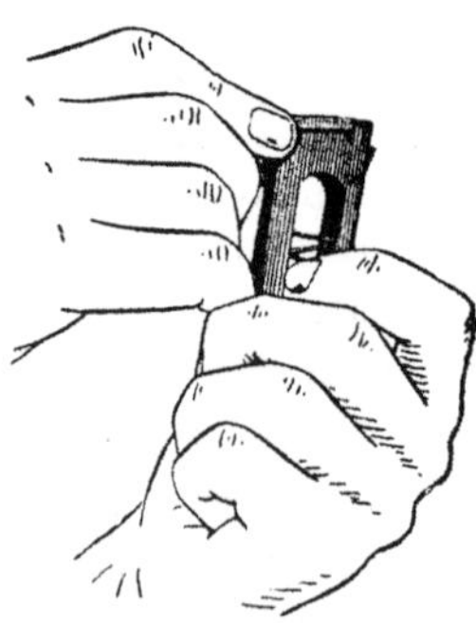

Figure 17. Disassembly of magazine.

i. Disassemble the magazine. Hold the magazine upside down in the left hand. With the thumb and index finger of the left hand, depress the magazine spring to relieve pressure on the floorplate. Using the right hand, remove the floorplate, magazine spring, and follower from the magazine body (figure 17).

13. Assembly of the pistol after complete disassembly is conducted in the reverse order:

a. Assemble the magazine. Hold the magazine body upside down in the left hand, so that the recess for the magazine catch is forward and up. With the right hand, insert the follower into the magazine. Place the spring into the magazine with the small (unbent) end down and, pressing on the spring with the thumb of the left hand (figure 18), with the right hand insert the floorplate into the formed edge so that the long (bent) end of the spring engages the slot in the floorplate.

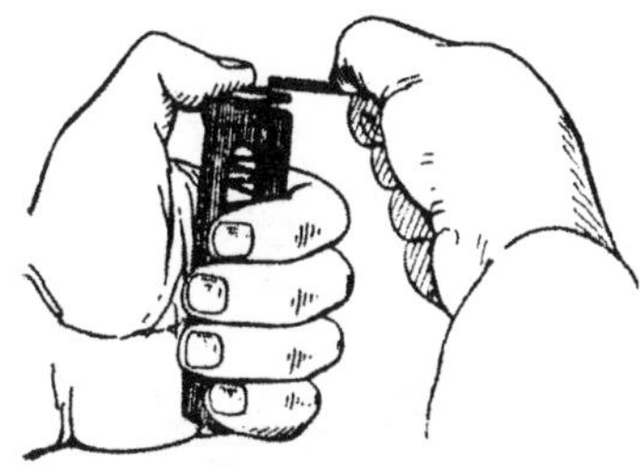

Figure 18. *Assembly of magazine.*

b. Install the extractor in the slide. Hold the slide in the left hand with the front toward you (figure 19). Use the right hand to insert the extractor spring into the groove of the slide, with the plunger outside. Place the extractor in the channel with the claw toward the recess in the slide. With the lug up, and holding it with the thumb of the left hand near the claw, carefully press the plunger into its seat with a drift. At the same time, pressing the extractor with the thumb of the left hand toward the plunger and down (rotating the claw around), engage its lug in the channel so that the head of the plunger drops in behind the recess of the lug.

c. Install the firing pin and safety in the slide. Hold the slide in the left hand with the back toward you, and insert the firing pin into the slide channel so that the notch toward the back is aligned with the hole for the safety. With the thumb and

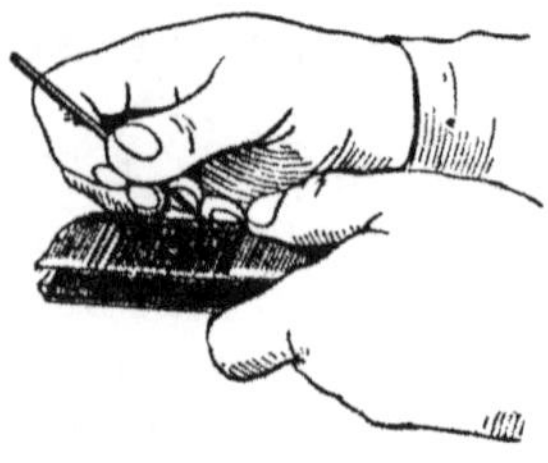

Figure 19. *Installing extractor into slide.*

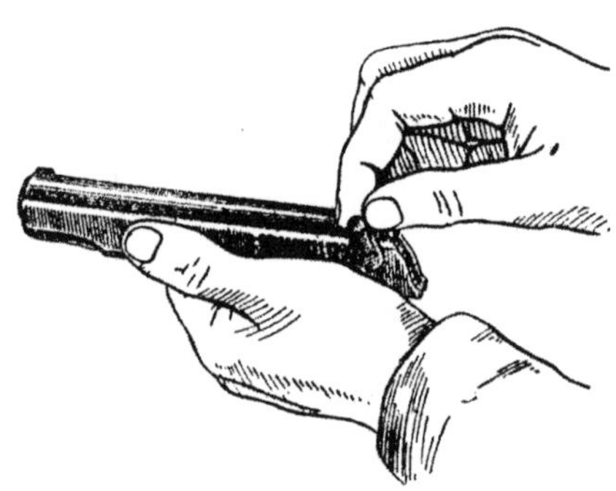

Figure 20. *Installing safety in slide.*

index finger of the right hand, insert the safety into its hole in the slide (figure 20), and rotate it downward as far as it will go.

d. Install the trigger in the receiver. Hold the receiver in the right hand. With the left hand, pull down on the forward portion of the trigger guard and move it sideways as was done during the partial disassembly of the pistol (paragraph 9). Insert the upper portion of the trigger into the opening in the receiver so that its pin can be installed in the mounting hole in the receiver. Return the forward end of the trigger guard to its normal position.

e. Install the trigger bar with cocking lever in the receiver. Hold the receiver in the left hand. Drawing the trigger to the rear, insert the pin of the trigger bar into the hole in the trigger and lower the rear end of the bar into the receiver at the rear of the handgrip frame.

f. Install the hammer in the receiver. Hold the receiver at the handgrip frame in the left hand with the trigger at its farthest forward position. Use the right hand to tilt the hammer forward, install its pin in the pinhole in the receiver (figure 21), and then return the hammer to the rear position.

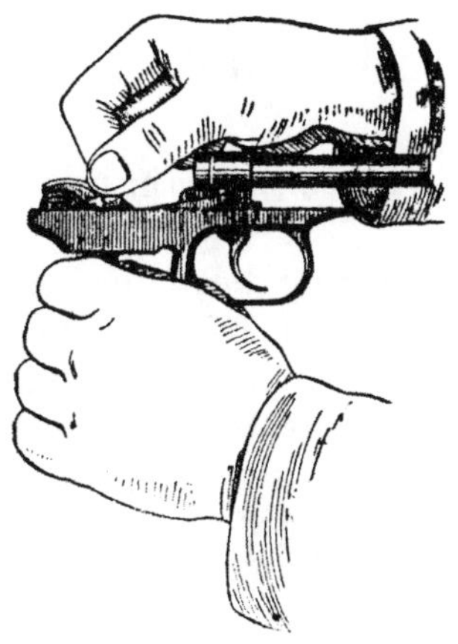

Figure 21. *Installation of hammer in receiver.*

g. Install the mainspring in the receiver and the handgrip on the handgrip frame. Hold the receiver in the left hand. Move the trigger forward and the cocking lever upward. With the right hand, insert the leaf of the mainspring into the opening in the receiver, and align the spring on the lug at the back of the handgrip frame (figure 22) so that the broad leaf of the mainspring is positioned in the depression of the hammer, and the narrow leaf is on the lug of the cocking lever. Verify the correctness of the positioning of the mainspring by lightly squeezing the trigger several times. If light pressure on the trigger causes the hammer to move rearward, the spring is

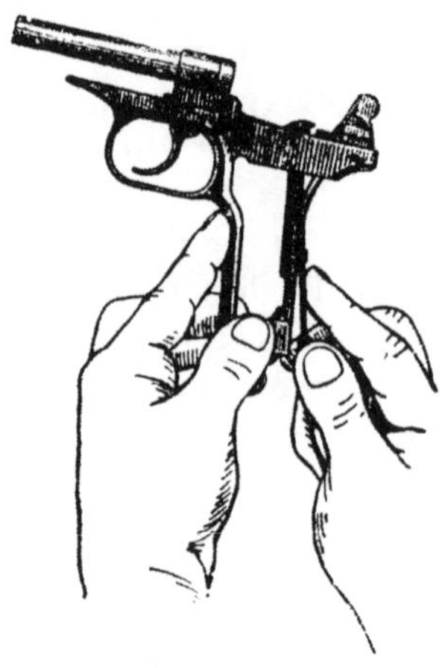

Figure 22. Installation of mainspring in receiver.

correctly installed. Keeping the mainspring in position, secure it with the latch. Install the handgrip on the handgrip frame and tighten the screw. Again, press on the trigger to insure that the mainspring remained in position during the installation of the handgrip.

Note: The hammer must not be cocked or released by pressure on the trigger while the sear and slide have not been installed on the receiver.

h. Install the slide stop and sear in the receiver. Hold the receiver in the left hand. With the right hand, insert the slide stop into the cutout in the receiver (figure 23). Hold the sear so that the flat on its right pin is turned forward. Then, slightly

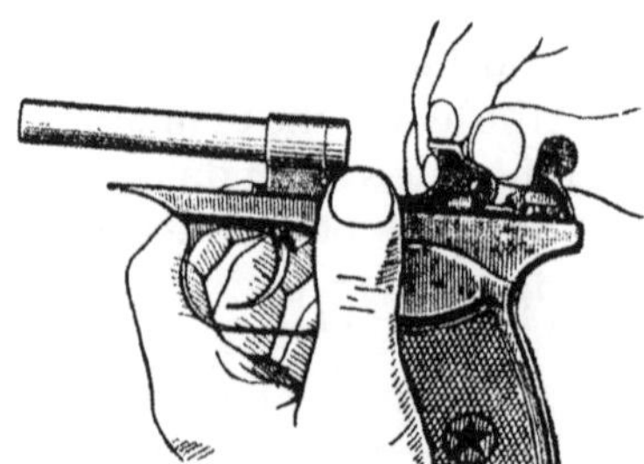

Figure 23. Installation of slide stop and sear in reciever.

raising the rear of the slide stop, insert the left pin of the sear (on which the spring is located) into its hole and insert the pin of the sear into the mounting hole in the receiver. Rotate the sear to the rear. With the end of the cleaning rod, raise the free end of the sear spring so that the trigger spring engages the lip of the slide stop.

i. Carry out subsequent assembly in accordance with the instructions in paragraph 10 above.

j. Verify proper functioning of the pistol after assembly in accordance with the instructions in paragraph 11 above.

Cleaning and lubricating the pistol

14. The pistol should always be kept clean and in good working order. This is achieved by timely and correct cleaning and lubricating, careful handling, and appropriate protection of the pistol.

15. The pistol should be cleaned:

— in combat, on maneuvers, and lengthy field exercises—daily during lulls in battle or during breaks between exercises;

— after firing—upon completion of firing (at a firing range, an indoor range, or in the field), clean the barrel with an alkaline solvent, then dry it and apply lubricant; after returning from firing, clean the pistol completely; within three to four days, clean the pistol again;

— if the pistol is not used—once every seven days.

16. Apply lubricant only on the clean and dry outer metal soon after cleaning, to prevent moisture from corroding the metal.

17. Officers will clean and lubricate their own pistols, unsupervised.

18. In a barracks or field camp environment, pistol cleaning is done in specially designated sites, on tables designed or made available for this purpose. In combat or on the march, cleaning is done on tentage, boards, plywood, or other surfaces that have been cleaned of dirt and dust.

19. The following items are used for bore-cleaning, overall cleaning, and lubricating the pistol:

— **alkaline solvent**—for neutralizing powder residues, and softening fouling in the barrel's lands and grooves and other components of the pistol that are exposed to the powder gases;

— **rifle oil**—for lubricating all metallic parts of the pistol; this lubricant helps the pistol's components and mechanisms function at temperatures down to +5 degrees C;

— **winter oil No. 21**—for lubricating the pistol's components during the winter; this lubricant supports functioning of the pistol's components and mechanisms at temperatures down to -40 degrees C;

— **gun lubricant**—for lubricating pistols placed in non-temporary storage;

— **clean cotton rags**—for wiping, cleaning, and lubricating pistol components, and also linen cord, free of lint, for cleaning the bore of the barrel.

20. The pistol is cleaned in the following manner:

a. **Prepare the cleaning and lubricating materials.**

b. **Inspect the cleaning rod**, as instructed in paragraph 60.

c. **Disassemble the pistol.**

d. Clean the bore of the barrel. Install a cleaning patch or cord through the hole on the cleaning rod end. The thickness of the patch should be such that the cleaning rod can pass through the barrel with a modest effort. Dip the patch in the alkaline solvent. Insert the cleaning rod into the barrel from the muzzle end. Place the receiver of the pistol on a table and hold it with the left hand. With the right hand, smoothly pass the cleaning rod back and forth several times through the entire length of the barrel. Replace the patch and, dipping it in the alkaline solvent, clean the barrel one more time. Carefully wipe the cleaning rod. Dry the bore of the barrel initially with the cord, and then with clean, dry patches. Inspect the patch. If it shows traces of residue or corrosion, swab the bore again with the cord dipped in the alkaline solvent, and then with dry cord and patches. Repeat this procedure until the patch comes out clean. Clean the chamber the same way. Carefully inspect the bore and chamber in the light. Pay special attention during the inspection to the chamber and the grooves of the rifling. No dirt or residue should remain in these areas.

Note. If the cleaning rod becomes stuck in the barrel during cleaning, drip some heating oil into the bore and, after several minutes, remove the cleaning rod. If the cleaning rod still will not come out, take the pistol to the weapon repair facility.

e. Clean the pistol's receiver with barrel and trigger guard. Clean and dry the components with cotton cloth to remove all dirt and residue. Remove corrosion with the cord or patches, dipped in alkaline solvent, then wipe completely dry. Use a wood stylus to aid in cleaning channels, grooves, and holes.

f. Clean the slide, recoil spring, slide stop, and components of the trigger mechanism. If the pistol is being cleaned after firing, clean the crevices of the slide with cord or patches dipped in alkaline solvent to remove all traces of powder residue. Wipe completely dry after cleaning. If the pistol was not fired, and there are no traces of corrosion or residue in the crevices of the slide, then wipe it with a dry cloth. Use a wooden stylus to aid in cleaning channels, grooves, and holes.

Wipe the remaining metal components dry with cotton to remove all traces of dirt and moisture, using the wooden stylus where needed.

After training or exercises without firing, clean the slide, slide stop, and components of the trigger mechanism without disassembling; after firing, or after exposing the pistol to rain or heavy dirt, disassemble for cleaning.

g. Wipe down the handgrip with a dry cloth.

h. Clean the magazine. After exercises or training, clean the magazine while assembled. After firing or exposing the pistol to rain or heavy dirt, disassemble the magazine to clean it. After training or exercises, clean and dry the magazine with a cloth to completely remove all moisture and dirt. After firing, use a cord or patch dipped in alkaline solvent. Wipe the follower dry after cleaning.

i. Wipe the holster inside and outside with a dry cloth to remove all dirt and moisture.

j. Wipe the cleaning rod dry.

21. Lubricate the pistol in the following manner:

a. Lubricate the bore of the barrel. Insert a cotton patch in the cleaning rod. Dip the patch in oil. Insert the rod in the barrel from the muzzle end and smoothly pass it through the entire length of the barrel two or three times, in order to cover the entire bore with a thin layer of oil. Lubricate the chamber from the breech end.

b. Lubricate the remaining metal components and mechanisms of the pistol. Lubricate the external surfaces with the aid of an oiled rag. Use an oiled patch over a wooden stylus to lubricate the channels, grooves, and holes. Apply lubricant in a thin, even layer. Excess lubricant on the pistol's components permits accumulation of dirt and can cause it to malfunction.

Do not lubricate the holster. Simply wipe it dry with a cloth.

c. Lubricate the cleaning rod.

d. When finished lubricating the pistol, assemble and inspect it. Verify that it has been correctly assembled and that the components and mechanisms function properly.

22. Lubricate the pistol's components and mechanisms in the winter (at temperatures below +5 degrees C) only with winter lubricant No. 21. During transition of the pistol to winter lubricant, carefully remove the rifle oil. If the rifle oil is not completely removed, the pistol will not function at freezing temperatures. Apply winter lubricant to the pistol's components and mechanisms in an even layer with an oiled cloth.

23. A pistol taken from freezing temperatures into a warm area need not be lubricated as long as it does not "sweat". When drops of moisture appear, immediately wipe the pistol's components and mechanisms dry and lubricate them.

24. When placed in non-temporary storage, the pistol should be carefully cleaned and liberally coated with gun oil or a mixture of 50 percent gun oil and 50 percent rifle oil.

Chapter 3

NOMENCLATURE AND FUNCTION OF THE PISTOL'S COMPONENTS AND MECHANISMS, AMMUNITION, AND ACCESSORIES

Nomenclature and function of the pistol's components and mechanisms

25. Receiver with barrel and trigger guard (figure 24).

The barrel guides the flight of the bullet. The bore of the barrel contains four lands and grooves, with a clockwise twist. The grooves impart a rotational spin to the bullet. The spaces between the grooves are called lands. The distance between two lands (in diameter) determines the caliber of the barrel's bore. For the Makarov, it is equal to 9 mm. The breech of the barrel is smooth and of greater diameter. It accommodates the cartridge and is called the chamber. The chamber has a shoulder. At the breech opening, a ramp guides the cartridge from the magazine into the chamber.

The external surface of the barrel is smooth. The recoil spring fits over the barrel.

The barrel is press fitted to the receiver and anchored with a pin.

A one-piece **receiver** houses all the pistol's components, including the handgrip frame.

The forward part of the receiver contains: upper—the platform that anchors the barrel, lower—the opening for the trigger guard and lug at its forward end. On the lateral sides of this opening are holes for the trigger mounting pin. The platform on the receiver contains: an opening on top where the barrel is press fitted and pinned; an opening below for accommodating the upper portion of the trigger; a curved channel for the forward pin of the trigger bar.

The back of the receiver contains: upper—shoulders with trunnion beds for the hammer and sear trunnions and with grooves for guiding the movement of the slide (trunnion beds

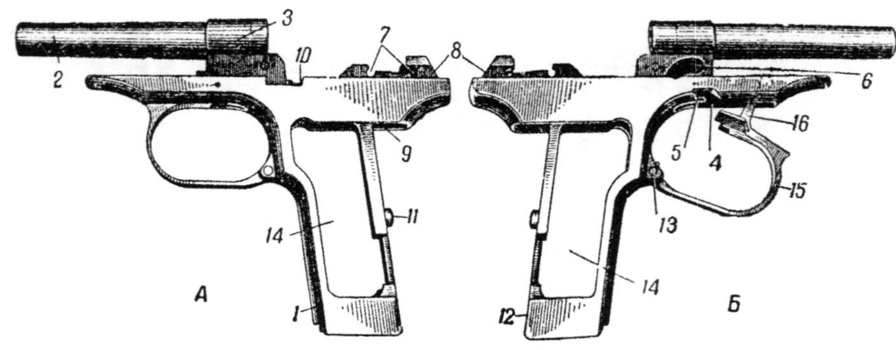

Figure 24. *Receiver with barrel and trigger guard.*
A - left side   B - right side

1 - *handgrip frame*	9 - *mainspring slot*
2 - *barrel*	10 - *slide stop cutout*
3 - *barrel base reinforcement*	11 - *mainspring and handgrip mounting boss*
4 - *trigger guard licking lug slot*	12 - *magazine release cutout*
5 - *trunnion bed for trigger*	13 - *trigger guard mounting boss*
6 - *trigger bar pin channel*	14 - *handgrip frame lateral cutouts*
7 - *trunnion beds for hammers and sear trunnions*	15 - *trigger guard*
8 - *slide rail channels*	16 - *slide locking lug*

have notches; in pistols produced beginning in 1953, the left trunnion bed of the sear does not have a notch); lower—an opening for the mainspring leaf.

The center portion of the receiver has an opening for the upper part of the magazine, and a cutout on the left wall for the slide stop.

The handgrip frame is the mounting point for the handgrip and the mainspring, and accommodates the magazine. It has: lateral cutouts (right and left) for reducing the pistol's weight; a lower opening for inserting the magazine into the handgrip; on the rear strap—a boss with threaded hole for mounting the mainspring and handgrip; below—a cutout for the magazine catch; on the forward strap—a channel with pin hole for mounting the trigger guard to the receiver with a pin.

The trigger guard protects the trigger from accidental firing. It has a lug at the forward end for limiting the movement of the slide during its rearward travel. The trigger guard is held in the receiver by a spring and a pin located on the front strap of the handgrip frame.

In pistols produced starting in 1954, the shape of the forward portion of the receiver was modified. The trigger guard and trigger were modified for better positioning of the trigger during firing. The shape of the opening on the bottom forward portion of the receiver was modified, along with the upper portion of the trigger guard that fits into that opening.

26. The **slide** (figure 25) delivers a cartridge from the magazine into the chamber, contains the barrel during firing, retains the cartridge, extracts the case, and moves the hammer to the cocked position.

Externally, the slide has: a front sight blade for aiming; a transverse groove for the rear sight; matting between the front and rear sights to prevent glare from the slide's upper surface during aiming; on the right side—an opening for the ejection of spent casings; a slot for the extractor; a seat for the extractor plunger and spring; on the left side—a seat for the safety and two notches for the safety latch: the upper—for the "safe" position, and the lower—for the "fire" position; at the upper notch a red dot, which is exposed when the safety is in the "fire"

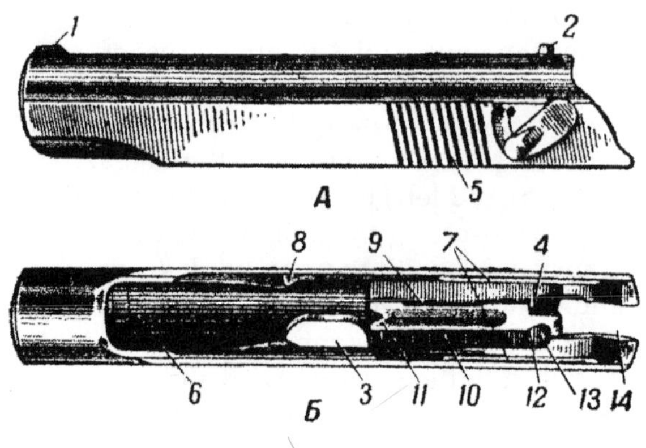

***Figure* 25.** *Slide.*
A - left side *B - bottom view*

1 - *front sight blade*
2 - *rear sight*
3 - *ejection port*
4 - *safety seat*
5 - *slide grip*
6 - *barrel and recoil spring channel*
7 - *slide rails*
8 - *slide stop lug*
9 - *extractor slot*
10 - *cocking lever tripping lug channel*
11 - *cartridge feed lug*
12 - *cocking lever sear disengagement boss*
13 - *cocking lever tripping lug recess*
14 - *hammer slot*

position, and covered when the safety is engaged; on both sides—grooves to comfortably grip the slide with the hand; at the back of the slide a slot housing the hammer.

Internally, the slide has: a channel accommodating the barrel and recoil spring; long rails to guide the slide on the receiver; a lug for placing the slide on the slide lock; a slot for the case ejector; a channel for the tripping lug of the cocking lever; a seat for holding the cartridge base; a feed lug to bring the cartridge from the magazine into the chamber; a boss to disengage the cocking lever lug from the sear; a recess to accommodate the disengaged lug of the cocking lever during the trigger pull; a groove housing the firing pin.

The **firing pin** (figure 26) serves to strike the primer. It has: at the front end—a striker; at the back end—a notch for the safety, which holds the firing pin in the groove of the slide.

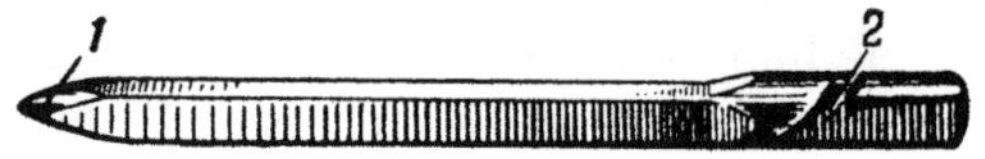

Figure 26. Firing pin.

1 - striker; 2 - safety notch

The firing pin is triangular, to reduce both its weight and working surfaces.

The **extractor** (figure 27) holds the cases (cartridges) in the seat of the slide prior to engaging the ejector. It has: a claw, which engages the rim of the case (cartridge) and holds it in the seat of the slide, and a lug for mounting the extractor in the slide; at the rear of the extractor lug is a notch to accommodate the nose of the plunger. At the rear of the extractor is a groove to facilitate prying the plunger during removal of the extractor from the slide. The extractor fits into a slot in the slide.

The front of the plunger is thickened. The front end of the extractor spring, which fits over the rear portion of the plunger

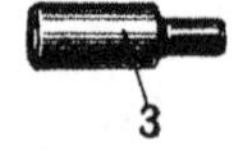

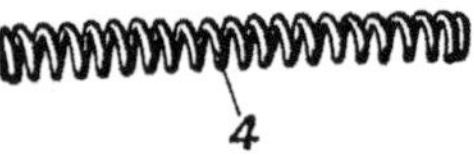

Figure 27. Extractor.

1 - extractor claw *2 - slide connecting lug*
3 - plunger *4 - extractor spring*

(smaller diameter), abuts the thickened part. The plunger with extractor spring fits into the slot in the slide. The claw of the extractor is always inclined toward the cartridge case seat under the pressure of the spring.

The **safety** (figure 28) allows safe handling of the pistol. It has: a thumb lever for moving the safety from the "fire" to the "safe" positions and back; a detent spring to hold the safety in the selected position; a shaft with a flange for rotating the sear and releasing the hammer from the sear during movement of the safety to the "safe" position; a catch for locking the hammer in the "safe" position; a lug for blocking the strike of the hammer when the safety is engaged.

The safety fits in a seat in the slide.

***Figure 28.** Safety.*

1 - thumb lever
2 - safety detent spring
3 - decocking flange
4 - slide locking shoulder
5 - hammer locking catch
6 - hammer blocking lug

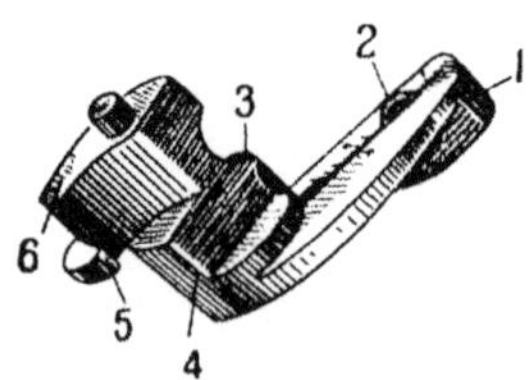

The **rear sight**, along with the front sight, is used to aim the weapon. It fits into a transverse channel on the slide.

27. The recoil spring (figure 29) returns the slide to the forward position after firing. One end of the spring has a smaller diameter coil than the other end. This coil fits snugly to the barrel during assembly, and insures that the spring stays on the barrel during disassembly of the pistol. The spring slides

Figure 29. *Recoil spring.*

over the barrel, and is positioned together with the barrel in the channel of the slide.

28. The firing mechanism (figure 30) consists of the hammer, sear with spring, trigger bar with cocking lever, trigger, mainspring, and mainspring retainer.

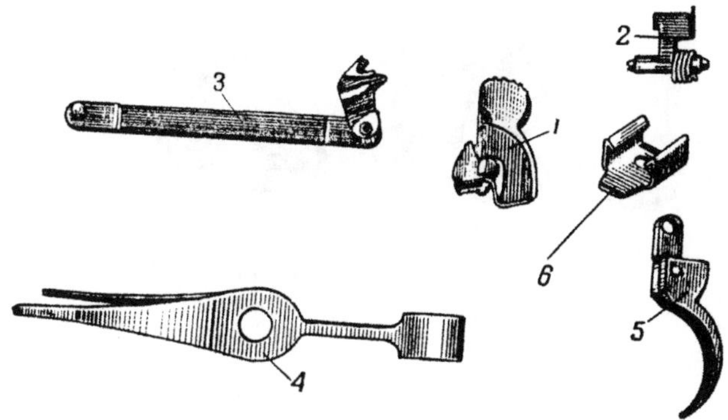

***Figure 30**. Components of the firing mechanism.*

1 - hammer
2 - sear with spring
3 - trigger bar with cocking lever
4 - mainspring
5 - trigger
6 - mainspring retainer

The **hammer** (figure 31) strikes the firing pin. It has: upper portion—grooved thumb spur for manual release of the hammer to the forward position; a recess permitting free movement of the hammer while uncocking; a groove for the safety detent; on the body of the hammer—two notches, the upper for the safety, and the lower for the sear; on the sides—trunnions on which the hammer rotates in the trunnion seats of the receiver, and arch-shaped areas where metal has been removed to save weight; on the right—the self-cocking lug for moving the hammer by the cocking lever; on the left—a notch for locking the hammer with the safety; lower portion—a recess for the broad leaf of the mainspring; on the right lower portion of the hammer body—a circular recess for the displacement of the cocking lever heel.

The hammer pins have flats for easy removal of the hammer from the receiver.

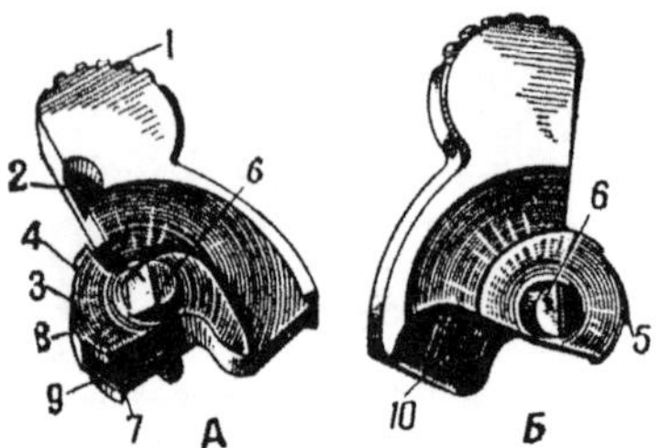

Figure 31. *Hammer*
A - left side *B - right side*

1 - grooved thumb spur
2 - hammer blocking lug recess
3 - safety detent groove
4 - safety notch
5 - sear notch
6 - hammer trunnion
7 - self-cocking lug
8 - hammer locking lug
9 - mainspring recess
10 - cocking lever heel recess

The **sear** (figure 32) holds the hammer at cock and safe positions. It has: trunnions, on which it rotates in the trunnion seats of the receiver; on the left—a claw for lifting the sear by the decocking flange of the safety during movement of the safety to the "safe" position; on the right—a detent on which the cocking lever acts during the lowering of the hammer.

On the left, the sear trunnion is secured by a spring, the free end of which is shaped like a hook to connect with the slide stop. The spring presses the end of the sear toward the hammer. The sear trunnions have flats for easy removal of the sear from the receiver.

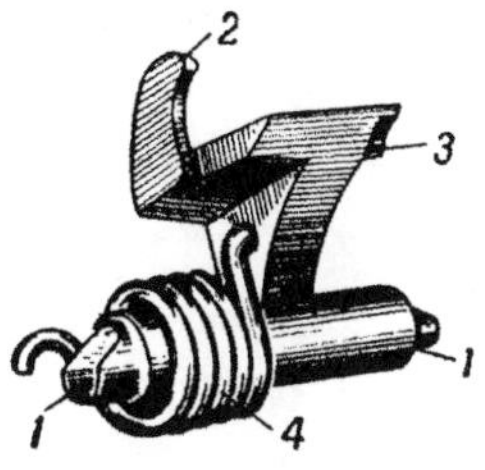

Figure 32. Sear

1 - sear trunnion
2 - decocking claw
3 - cocking lever detent
4 - sear spring

The **trigger bar with cocking lever** (figure 33) lowers the hammer from full cock and cocks the hammer when pressure is applied to the trigger.

The trigger bar has pins on the ends. The front pin fits into the upper arm of the trigger, and the rear pin joins with the cocking lever.

The cocking lever has: a tripping lug, that uncouples it from the sear during the rearward movement of the slide; a cutout for the sear detent; the double-action lug, which cocks the hammer when pressure is applied to the trigger; a heel, on which rests

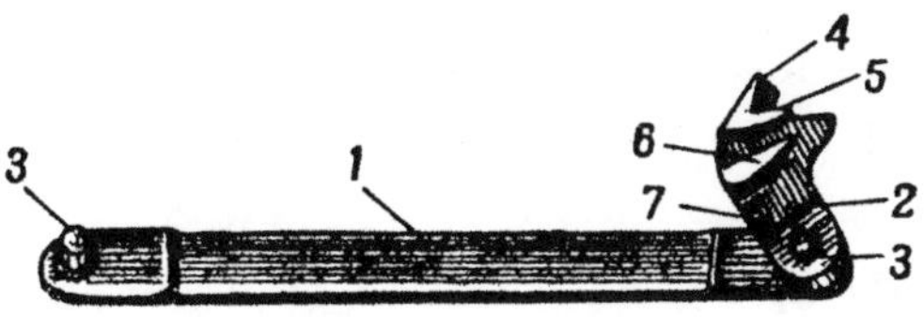

***Figure** 33. Trigger bar with cocking lever.*

1 - trigger bar 2 - cocking lever 3 - trigger bar connecting pin
4 - cocking lever tripping lug 5 - sear detent cutout
6 - double action lug 7 - cocking lever heel

the narrow leaf of the mainspring. The heel of the cocking lever rests in a circular recess of the hammer.

The **trigger** (figure 34) releases the hammer from cock and cocks the hammer. It has: trunnions, that rest in the trunnion wells of the receiver; a hole linking the trigger with the trigger bar; and the finger piece.

The upper end of the trigger fits into the opening of the receiver front.

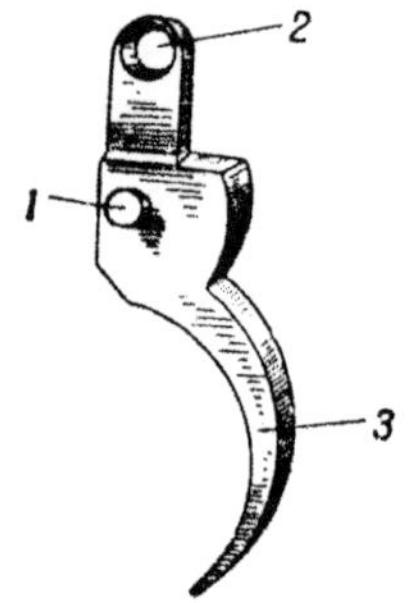

Figure 34. Trigger.

1 - trunnion
2 - trigger bar connecting hole
3 - finger piece

The **mainspring** (figure 35) drives the hammer and cocking lever. It has: a broad leaf for operating the hammer; a narrow leaf for operating the cocking lever and trigger bar; in the middle sector—a hole for mounting the spring on the threaded boss of the handgrip frame. The lower end of the mainspring is the magazine catch. The end of the wide leaf of the mainspring is curved to permit "releasing" the hammer, that is, to place the hammer in a safe, lowered position. The mainspring is secured on the handgrip frame by a retainer and screw.

Figure 35. Mainspring.

1 - wide leaf
2 - narrow leaf
3 - spring mounting hole
4 - magazine catch

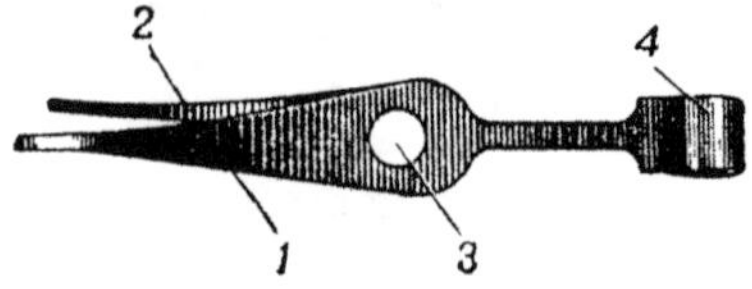

29. The **handgrip with screw** (figure 36) covers the lateral cutouts of the handgrip frame and makes gripping the pistol comfortable. The one-piece handgrip has: a hole for the screw that secures the handgrip to the handgrip frame; a lanyard loop; channels for mounting the handgrip on the handgrip frame; in the rear wall of the handgrip is a cutout for the magazine catch. A metal sleeve with a shoulder is fitted in the screw hole to prevent the screw head from loosening. The handgrip is made of plastic.

The handgrip mounting screw secures the mainspring and the handgrip to the handgrip frame. It has a head and a threaded shaft.

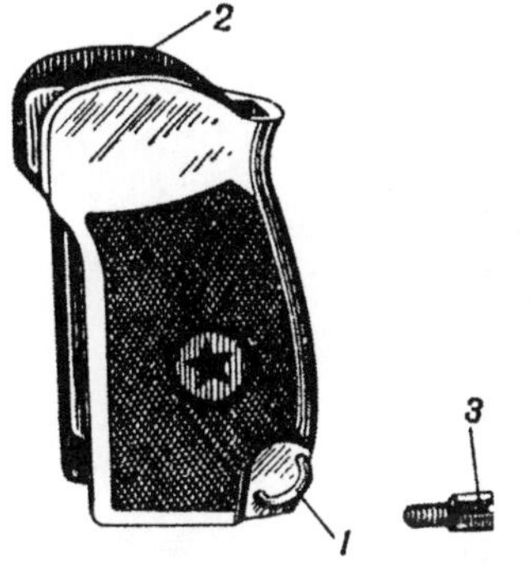

Figure 36. *Handgrip with screw*

1 - *lanyard loop*
2 - *frame channel*
3 - *handgrip screw*

30. The **slide stop** (figure 37) holds the slide in the rear position after all rounds have been fired from the magazine. It has: at the front—the slide stop lug; a knurled plunger for releasing the slide with thumb pressure; at the rear—a hole for joining with the left trunnion of the sear; above—an ejector for ejecting the cases (cartridges) through the port in the slide.

The slide stop is mounted in the left wall of the receiver.

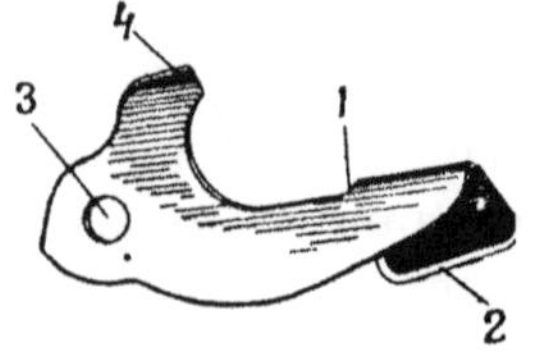

Figure 37. Slide stop.

1 - slide stop lug
2 - knurled plunger
3 - left sear trunnion hole
4 - ejector

31. The **magazine** (figure 38) holds eight cartridges. It consists of the body, the follower, the follower spring, and the floor plate.

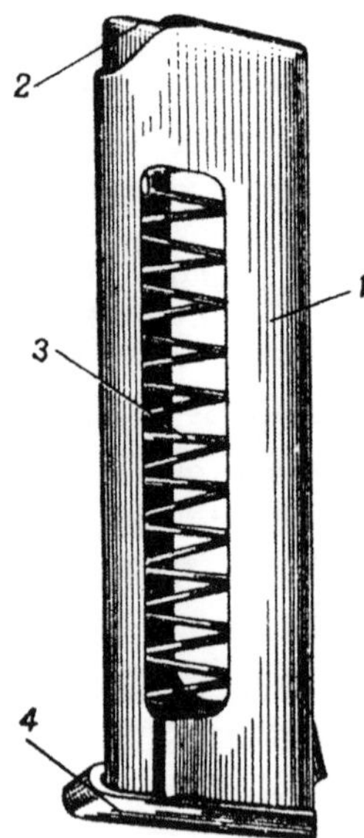

Figure 38. Magazine

1 - body
2 - follower
3 - follower spring
4 - floor plate

The **magazine body** (figure 39) holds all of the magazine's parts. The upper edge of the side walls are bent inward to hold the cartridges and follower, and also to direct the cartridges into the chamber during their delivery by the slide motion. It has: in the lateral walls—cutouts to reduce weight and to indicate the number of rounds remaining in the magazine; on the bottom—rolled edges to hold the magazine floorplate, a lug for the magazine catch, a cutout for unhindered movement of the left side of the magazine floorplate, and a raised slot for passage of the follower catch.

The magazine is inserted into the handgrip through the lower opening on the handgrip frame.

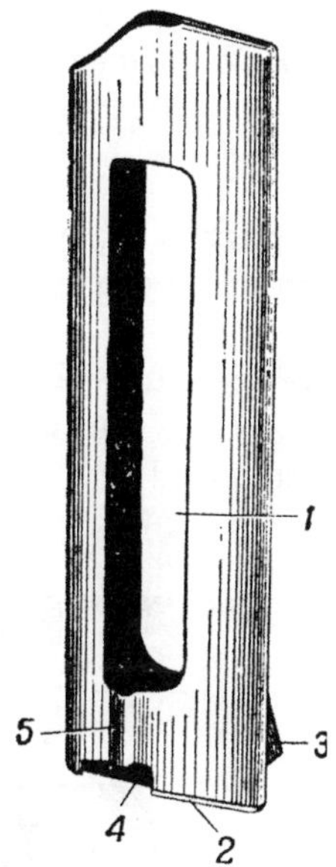

Figure 39*. Magazine body.*

1 - side cutouts
2 - rolled edges for floor plate
3 - magazine catch lug
4 - magazine floor plate cutout
5 - magazine follower catch slot

The **magazine follower** (figure 40) pushes the cartridges upward. It has two pressed ends that control the movement of the follower in the magazine body. On the left side of one of the pressed ends is a catch for engaging the slide stop when all the cartridges have been expended from the magazine.

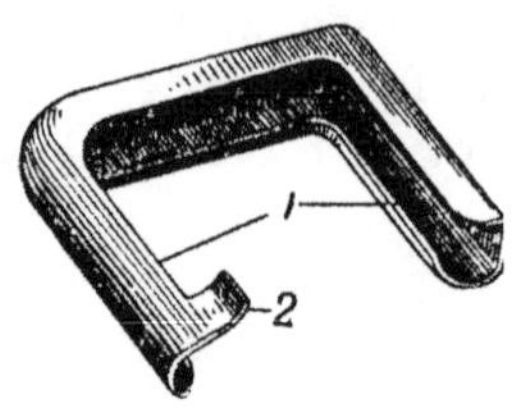

Figure 40. Magazine follower.

The **follower spring** (figure 41) applies upward pressure on the follower. The lower end of the spring is bent to engage the magazine floorplate.

The **magazine floorplate** (figure 42) has a hole for the bent lower end of the follower spring, and grooves that fit onto the rolled edges of the magazine body.

Figure 41. Magazine follower spring.

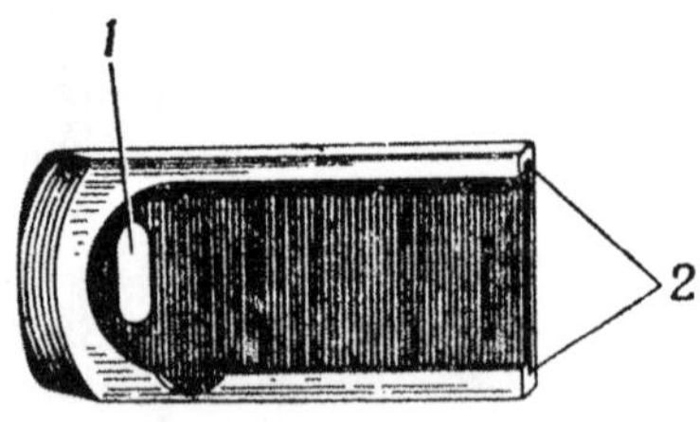

Figure 42. Magazine floorplate.

1 - *magazine follower spring hole*
2 - *floor plate mounting grooves*

Nomenclature and function of the accessory (cleaning rod)

32. The **accessory** (cleaning rod) is used for disassembly, assembly, cleaning, and lubricating the pistol.

The cleaning rod (figure 43) has: on one end—an opening for holding a patch or cord, on the other—a ring for holding the cleaning rod during cleaning. The circular end of the cleaning rod has a flat screwdriver blade for removing and replacing the handgrip screw during disassembly and assembly of the pistol.

Cleaning rods issued since 1955 have the screwdriver flat positioned differently, and on the end of the shaft is a special protrusion intended for facilitating removal and replacement of the extractor.

Figure 43. Accessory cleaning rod.

1 - patch holder slot
2 - screwdriver tip

Functioning of the cartridge

33. The **9-mm pistol cartridge** (figure 44) consists of the case, the primer, the propellant, and the projectile.

The **case** contains the propellant and joins together all the components of the cartridge. It protects the propellant and primer. During firing, it prevents the escape of gases from the bore of the barrel through the chamber.

At the bottom of the case are: the primer pocket; the anvil, against which the firing pin strikes the primer; and two priming holes, through which the flames from the ignited primer travel to the propellant. The outside of the case bottom is rimmed for engaging the extractor claw.

The **projectile** consists of a lead core pressed into a steel plated copper and zinc alloy jacket. The projectile is secured in the case by a tight crimp.

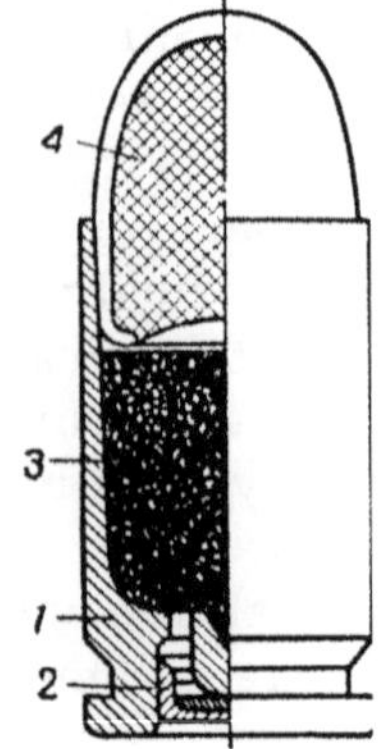

Figure 44. 9-mm pistol cartridge.

1 - casing
2 - primer
3 - propellant charge
4 - projectile

The **propellant** consists of a smokeless gunpowder charge.

The **primer** ignites the propellant charge.

The primer consists of a brass cap with a striker pressed into it, and a stannic disk that covers a striker.

During the strike of the firing pin, the striker is ignited and yields a powerful flame.

34. The cartridges for loading the pistol are supplied by a single-row 8-round magazine. The magazine is loaded by inserting the cartridges and pushing down on them manually.

35. The cartridges are packed in a standard wooden cartridge crate of 2560 rounds. Each crate holds two soldered galvanized tin bricks that contain cartridges in cardboard packages, 16 cartridges in each package. A single galvanized tin brick holds 80 cardboard packages.

Printed on the sides of the wooden crate are the noun nomenclature of the ammunition in the crate, the lot number of the ammunition, the manufacturing facility, the type and lot number of the propellant, and the number of rounds in the crate.

A single crate of cartridges weighs approximately 33 kg (73 pounds).

Chapter 4

FUNCTION OF THE PISTOL'S COMPONENTS AND MECHANISMS

Condition of the pistol's components and mechanisms before loading

36. The pistol's components and mechanisms are in the following condition before loading.

The **slide**, under the force of the recoil spring, is at its most forward position; the cartridge case seat is up against the breech cutout of the barrel, and the barrel is secured by the free slide. The longitudinal slide rails fit in the channels in the rear portion of the receiver. The slide is locked to the receiver by a shoulder on the safety.

The **hammer** is released under the force of the mainspring broad leaf and is held by its forward plane on the safety catch so that it cannot be moved forward.

The **sear** is raised by the flange on the shaft of the safety and held in this position so that there is a small clearance between the safety cock of the hammer and the end of the sear.

The **trigger bar with cocking lever** is at its most rearward position under the tension of the mainspring narrow leaf; the cocking lever is seated in the frame and its double-action detent is engaged with the self-cocking lug of the hammer so that the hammer does not move during the trigger pull, but has some free rearward movement.

The **magazine** is in the handgrip. The follower is at the top and pressing against the lower surface of the slide. The catch on the follower is pressing on the slide stop.

The **thumb safety** is in the "safe" position. In this position the safety lug is in the downward position and is in contact with the forward surface of the hammer; the flange on the safety shaft raises the sear up and holds it in this position; the safety catch fits into the notch of the hammer and, engaging it, holds the hammer in the "safe" position so that it cannot be cocked;

the shoulder of the safety fits into a notch on the left side of the receiver and locks the slide with the receiver.

Function of the pistol's components and mechanisms during loading

37. To load the pistol, it is necessary to:

— load the magazine with cartridges;

— insert the magazine into the handgrip;

— take the weapon off "safe" (rotate the thumb safety downward);

— pull the slide to its most rearward position and sharply release it.

When loading the magazine, place the cartridges on the follower one on top of the other in a single row, pressing down on the follower spring; as cartridges are inserted into the magazine, the spring compresses. The uppermost cartridge is held by the bent edges of the magazine body side walls.

When the loaded magazine is inserted into the handgrip of the pistol, the magazine catch engages the lug on the magazine spine and holds the magazine in the handgrip. The uppermost cartridge is pressed against the bottom of the slide. The follower is pressed down and its catch is not in contact with the slide stop.

When putting the weapon off "safe" (rotate the thumb safety downward), the safety lug is raised upward, freeing the hammer. The hammer rotates on its trunnion under the tension of the mainspring broad leaf, and its head moves forward until the safety notch disengages from the end of the sear. During rotation of the safety, its catch, coming out of the notch on the hammer, is freed from the hammer, which permits the free movement of the hammer to the rear. During the rotation of the safety, the safety shoulder withdraws from the left cutout on the receiver and disconnects the slide from the receiver. This permits the slide to be drawn to the rear with the hand.

While the slide is being drawn to the rear:

The slide, moving along the longitudinal channels of the receiver, rotates the hammer rearward. Under the pressure of the mainspring, the sear drops its end behind the cocking lug of the hammer. The rearward movement of the slide is limited by the lug at the forward end of the trigger guard.

The hammer, during the rotation of the forward portion of the cocking lever recess, engages the trigger bar with the cocking lever forward and somewhat raised, which also removes the slack from the trigger. When the cocking lever is raised, its cutout matches the detent of the sear.

The magazine follower, under the pressure of the follower spring, raises the cartridges upward so that the uppermost cartridge is positioned in front of the cartridge feed lug.

When the slide is released, the recoil spring sends the slide forward. Moving along the longitudinal channels of the receiver, the cartridge feed lug catches the uppermost cartridge and pushes it into the chamber. The cartridge, sliding between the bent edges of the magazine sidewalls and onto the ramp of the barrel breech, enters the chamber and is held at the front edge of the casing in the recess of the chamber; the barrel is fixed by the free slide.

When the slide reaches its most forward position and has delivered the cartridge into the chamber, the extractor claw engages the casing's rear rim.

The hammer is cocked.

The pistol is ready to fire (figure 45).

Function of the components and mechanisms of the loaded pistol when the safety is disengaged

38. If the pistol does not have to be fired, the safety can be engaged without lowering the hammer from the cocked position by rotating the thumb safety upward so that the red dot is covered.

When the thumb safety is rotated, the flange engages a detent on the sear, causing the sear to rotate and free the hammer. The hammer rotates under the pressure of the mainspring broad leaf. The safety detent is released and permits the hammer to drop. The rotating safety shoulder fits into a recess on the left side of the receiver and locks the slide to the receiver. When lowered, the thumb safety fits into a notch on the hammer and locks it, so that the hammer cannot be cocked.

If the safety is released on a loaded pistol, the hammer

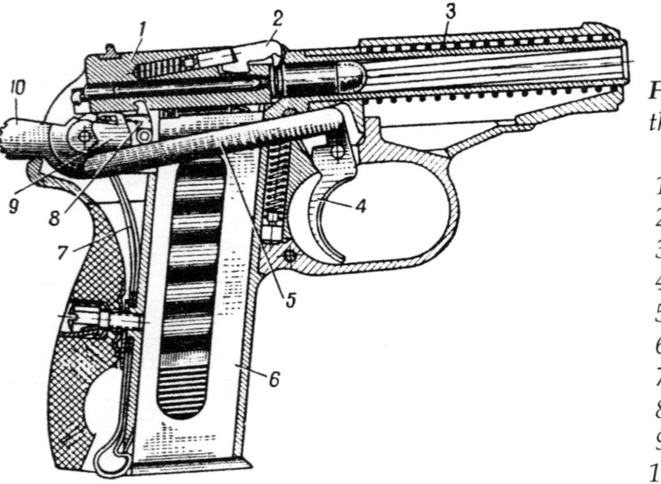

Figure 45. *Position of components and mechanisms of the pistol before firing.*

1 - *slide*
2 - *extractor*
3 - *extractor spring*
4 - *trigger*
5 - *trigger bar*
6 - *magazine*
7 - *mainspring*
8 - *sear with spring*
9 - *cocking lever*
10 - *hammer*

automatically remains at safe due to this decocking feature. In this case, the pistol is ready for immediate double-action firing. [In other words, the hammer is forward and must be cocked by pulling the trigger.] If the pistol is subjected to accidental blows or is dropped, it remains safe because of the automatic dropping of the hammer to the decock position.

The hammer may be dropped without using the safety. By squeezing the trigger with the right forefinger and lowering the hammer with the right thumb, the hammer is automatically at the decock position upon release of the trigger. [This procedure, however, is not recommended.]

Function of the pistol's components and mechanisms during firing

39. In order to fire, one must release the safety, cock the hammer, and squeeze the trigger.

When releasing the safety and cocking the hammer, the pistol's components and mechanisms function as explained in paragraph 37.

When squeezing the trigger, the trigger bar displaces forward, and the cocking lever on the rear end of the trigger bar rotates on its shaft. It raises upward until it no longer engages the sear (preliminary drop). Then the cocking lever raises the sear and disengages it from the cocked hammer. The tripping lug of the cocking lever fits into a recess in the top of the slide.

The hammer is freed from the sear, and drops sharply forward on its shaft under the pressure of the mainspring broad leaf and strikes the firing pin.

The firing pin is driven sharply forward and strikes the cartridge primer with the striker, firing the shot.

Gas pressure drives the projectile forward through the bore. At the same time, the gases push against the walls and base of the case. The case expands and completely presses against the chamber wall. The gas pressure on the bottom of the case transfers to the slide, driving it rearward.

Function of the pistol's components and mechanisms after firing

40. The pressure of the propellant gases on the case base forces the slide to the rear along with the fired case. As it starts rearward (three to five millimeters from start of movement), the slide displaces the tripping lug of the cocking lever to the right, thus uncoupling it from the sear.

The freed sear, under the pressure of the spring, presses against the hammer. When the hammer rotates rearward, the end of the sear engages the hammer's cocking lug and holds it until the next shot.

During the slide's subsequent rearward movement, the tripping lug of the cocking lever moves along the channel of the slide. The case, held by the extractor against the face of the slide, strikes the ejector and is thrown out through the port in the slide wall.

The magazine follower raises the next cartridge and places it in front of the cartridge feed lug on the bottom of the slide.

The slide, reaching its most rearward position, returns forward under the pressure of the return spring. It catches the next cartridge from the magazine and chambers it. When the slide reaches its most forward position and has chambered the round, the extractor claw engages the case rim.

The cocking lever engages the sear (from the side), and its tripping lug is positioned against the channel in the slide. The pistol is prepared for the next shot.

41. To fire the next round, one must release the trigger and squeeze it again.

When the trigger is released, the trigger bar with cocking lever returns to its normal position under pressure from the mainspring narrow leaf, while the cocking lever drops downward and its sear detent cutout engages the sear.

When the trigger is squeezed, the cocking lever raises the sear and again frees the hammer from the sear. The next shot is fired.

If the slide does not return to its most forward position (indicating all cartridges are expended), then the tripping lug of the cocking lever does not engage the recess in the slide. As a result, the cocking lever does not engage the sear. If the trigger is subsequently squeezed, the sear does not rotate and the hammer does not drop. This excludes the possibility of firing if a cartridge is not fully chambered.

Function of the pistol's components and mechanisms during double-action firing

42. When firing is conducted without preliminary cocking of the hammer, the hammer is automatically cocked when the trigger is squeezed (figure 46). In this case, the cocking lever, engaged by its double-action lug with the self-cocking lug on the hammer, cocks the hammer. The hammer, not held by the sear, separates from the self-cocking lug and strikes the firing pin, firing the shot.

Function of the pistol's components and mechanisms upon expenditure of all the cartridges from the magazine

43. When all the cartridges in the magazine are expended, the catch on the magazine follower raises the forward end of the slide stop. The slide, caught by its lug on the raised portion of the slide stop, remains in the rearward position.

The hammer is cocked.

The magazine follower spring is exerting its least pressure. The slide, held on the slide stop, remains in the rearward position when the magazine is released from the handgrip.

44. The slide is freed from the slide stop (upon removal or insertion of the magazine) by pressing with the thumb on the slide stop.

Figure 46. *Position of the pistol's components and mechanisms before double-action firing.*

1 - slide
2 - extractor
3 - recoil spring
4 - trigger
5 - trigger bar
6 - magazine
7 - mainspring
8 - sear
9 - cocking lever
10 - hammer

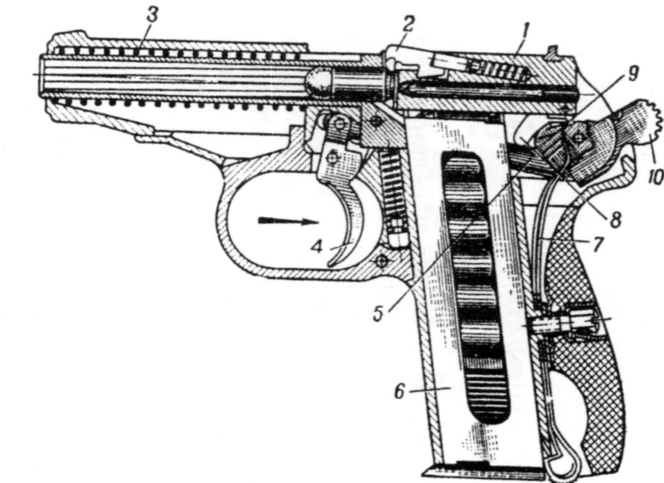

Chapter 5

PREVENTING AND CLEARING STOPPAGES DURING PISTOL FIRING

45. With proper handling, attentive maintenance, and lubrication, the pistol is a reliable and dependable weapon.

However, after prolonged use, as a result of component and mechanism wear, but more often due to careless handling and inattentive maintenance, the pistol can malfunction, resulting in stoppages during firing.

46. To prevent stoppages and to maintain dependable operation of the pistol, one must:

— correctly prepare the pistol for firing;

— inspect, clean and lubricate the pistol in a timely manner and observing all the regulations. One must particularly and carefully clean and oil the pistol's working components;

— inspect the ammunition before firing. Incorrect, corroded, and dirty cartridges should not be fired;

— protect the pistol against dirt and accidental drops during firing and while traveling;

— clean, inspect, and lubricate the pistol at the first opportunity in combat or during prolonged firing;

— if, before firing, the pistol has been subjected to prolonged cold temperatures, then before loading it, briskly pull and release the slide several times, squeezing the trigger each time.

47. If a stoppage occurs during firing, attempt to recharge the pistol [chamber another cartridge]. If recharging the pistol does not clear the stoppage, then the cause of the stoppage must be determined, and corrected as indicated in the following table.

Stoppage	Cause of Stoppage	Corrective Action
1. **Misfire:** slide at most forward position, hammer released, but pistol did not fire.	a. Malfunctioning primer, with deep indentation from firing pin.	a. Recharge pistol and continue to fire.
	b. Accumulation of oil or fouling of firing pin and hammer.	b. Inspect and clean pistol.
	c. Handgrip screw not fully tightened (in pistols without mainspring retainer).	c. Retighten screw in handgrip.
2. **Round not fully chambered by slide:** slide stops, does not close completely; trigger cannot be squeezed.	a. Dirty chamber and receiver channels. b. Extractor moves with difficulty due to fouled spring and plunger.	Send slide forward by striking the rear of the slide with the palm, and continue to fire. Inspect and clean pistol.
3. **Failure to feed ammunition from magazine into chamber:** slide in forward position, but no round in chamber; slide stopped midway with cartridge, but failed to chamber it.	a. Dirty magazine and pistol moving parts.	a. Recharge pistol and continue to fire. Clean pistol and magazine.
	b. Deformation of upper lips of magazine body.	b. Replace deformed magazine with spare.

Stoppage	Cause of Stoppage	Corrective Action
4. **Failure of slide to extract (jammed) case:** case not ejected through ejection port and is caught between slide and breech.	a. Dirty moving parts. b. Broken extractor or extractor spring.	a. Remove jammed case and continue firing. b. Remove extractor and spring and inspect; if extractor or spring is broken, turn pistol in to repair facility.

Chapter 6

INSPECTION, PREPARATION OF THE PISTOL AND AMMUNITION FOR FIRING,AND MAINTENANCE AND STORAGE OF THE PISTOL

General Conditions

48. Periodic inspection of the pistol is conducted at intervals specified by the Internal Service Regulation to determine its condition, functionality, and combat readiness.

Inspection of the pistol is conducted in assembled or disassembled form. The degree of disassembly is determined prior to each inspection.

The holster, spare magazine, and cleaning rod are inspected simultaneously with the inspection of the pistol.

49. Each serviceman armed with the pistol should inspect his pistol **daily, prior to departure for exercises, prior to firing, and during cleaning.**

Before departing on maneuvers and immediately before firing, inspect the pistol in assembled form, and during cleaning—in disassembled and assembled form.

50. Check the following during daily inspection of the pistol:

— are there deposits of rust, dirt, scratches, pitting, or cracks on the metal components; what is the condition of the lubricant?

— do the slide, magazine, trigger mechanism, safety, and slide stop operate properly?

— are the front and rear sights serviceable?

— is the magazine held in the handgrip properly?

— is the bore clean?

Deficiencies in the pistol should be corrected immediately. If they cannot be corrected at the unit level, the pistol must be turned in to a repair facility.

Inspection of the pistol in assembled form

51. When inspecting the pistol in assembled form, check the following:

a. Are there any traces of corrosion, scratches, pitting, or cracks on the pistol's components? Do the numbers on the slide, safety, and magazines correspond to the number on the receiver?

b. Is there any pitting on the sights that would interfere with aiming? Are the sights firmly bedded in the slide and does the alignment mark on the rear sight correspond with the mark on the slide?

c. Can the thumb safety be manipulated easily from one position to the other, and is it firmly attached when the slide is fully open or fully closed?

d. Does the hammer "decock": during lowering of the hammer and cocking it back with the trigger, the hammer should be able to be pushed forward by finger pressure, and after pressure is released, it should return energetically to the initial position; during release of the trigger and upon stopping the pressure on the hammer, the hammer should be at safe cock, and in this position a moderate amount of pressure should not be able to dislodge it from safe cock and displace it forward.

e. Is the trigger guard securely mounted in the receiver and can its forward end be twisted to the side in order to remove the slide?

f. Is the handgrip mounting screw tight?

g. Are there dirt, traces of corrosion, or other defects in the bore? (This can be determined by locking the slide open on the slide stop and inspecting the bore from the muzzle end. Insure that the pistol is unloaded.)

h. Are there any dents in the walls or upper edges of the magazine, and does the follower move easily inside the magazine?

i. Can the magazine be inserted into and removed from the handgrip easily, and does the magazine catch hold it securely?

j. Do the pistol's components and mechanisms work properly? To verify this, do the following procedure:

Place the thumb safety in the "fire" position (downward), draw the slide back with the hand and release it. The slide, having returned slightly forward, should be held to the rear by the slide stop. Press on the slide stop. The slide should return sharply to the forward position under the pressure of the recoil spring, and the hammer should remain cocked. Squeeze the trigger. The hammer should release and strike the firing pin.

Remove the magazine from the pistol's handgrip and load it with training cartridges. Insert the magazine into the handgrip, pull the slide to the rear and release it. Under the pressure of the recoil spring, the slide should go all the way forward and chamber a cartridge. Manual operation of the slide should result in the cartridge being sharply ejected through the ejection port.

Rotate the thumb safety upward to the "safe" position. The hammer should disengage from the cocked position, strike the safety lug, and remain in a somewhat rearward position. The slide should now be locked, the hammer should not be able to be cocked either by direct manipulation with the thumb or by squeezing the trigger (self cocking).

Place the thumb safety in the "fire" position and squeeze the trigger. The hammer should rotate to full cock, then without pause rotate forward to strike the firing pin.

Place the hammer at full cock and press rearward on the head of the hammer. It should not be released from full cock. Then squeeze the trigger. The hammer should release from full cock and sharply strike the firing pin.

k. Is the hammer blocked by the safety lug during rotation of the safety before the sear begins to lift? Conduct the inspection in the following manner.

Place the hammer at full cock. Hold the pistol in the right hand with the muzzle down and observe the sear through the opening in the slide. With the right thumb, slowly move the safety upward until the sear begins to lift. Having determined the position of the safety at the moment of the sear's lifting (that is, at the moment of contact of the safety shoulder flange with the sear catch), hold the hammer with the right thumb, squeeze but do not release the trigger with the middle finger, and slowly lower the hammer to the forward position. The hammer should be caught by the safety lug, that is, it should be blocked by the safety (figure 47).

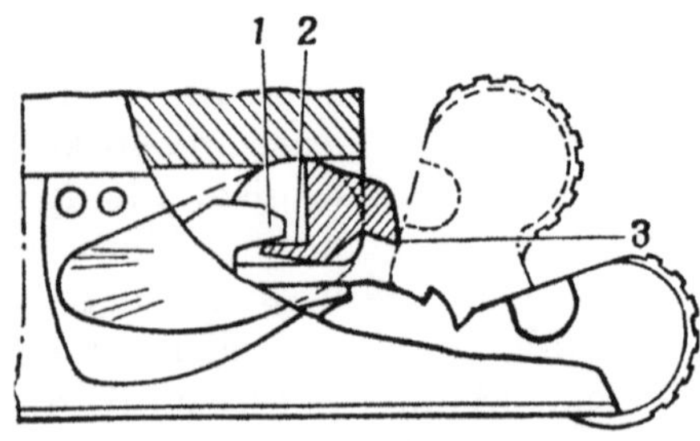

Figure 47. Sketch of hammer blocked by safety lug.
1 - decocking claw
2 - safety decocking flange
3 - hammer blocking lug

Inspection of the pistol in disassembled form

52. When disassembled, each of the pistol's components and mechanisms is closely inspected individually to ascertain if any metal is deteriorating, if threads are damaged, if there are scratches, pitting, or eruptions, if any part is bent, corroded, or dirty, and if all parts have the same number.

53. When inspecting the slide, barrel, and trigger guard, pay special attention to the condition of the bore.

Inspect the bore from both the muzzle and breech ends. Check the cleanliness of the bore and chamber, and the appearance of the breech.

The bore and chamber can be chromed or unchromed.

During inspection of an unchromed bore, the following deficiencies can be observed.

Eruption — the initial breakdown of the metal by corrosion. An eruption has the appearance of points and spots in different locations or on the entire surface of the bore.

Corrosion — a dark deposit on the metal. Corrosion that cannot be seen with the naked eye can be detected by wiping the bore with a clean patch, on which the corrosion will leave yellow deposits.

Effects of corrosion — dark shallow spots which remain after removal of corrosion.

Pitting — significant depressions in the metal, resulting from prolonged corrosive action. The removal of pitting is prohibited at the unit level.

Copper fouling — occurs during the firing of bullets jacketed with copper/zinc alloy. Copper fouling appears as light copper deposits on the walls of the bore. It can be removed only in the weapon repair facility.

Scratches — lines, sometimes with noticeable raising of the metal at the edges.

Dents — with greater and lesser noticeable depths, sometimes with a raising of the metal.

Rounding of the corners of the lands in the bore — especially noticeable on the left edge of the lands.

The Instructions for Classification of Artillery Armaments governs the determination of the qualitative condition of the chromed bores.

Removal of scratches from the bores is not permitted.

54. When inspecting the slide with extractor, firing pin, and safety, pay special attention to the condition of the internal recesses, seats, and protrusions, which should not be fouled. Insure that the firing pin moves freely in the slide channel, that the extractor is forcefully pressed toward the face of the slide and its claw is not chipped.

55. When inspecting the recoil spring, insure that it has no burred edges, corrosion, kinks, dirt, or cracks.

56. When inspecting the components of the trigger mechanism, pay particular attention to the condition of the hammer, sear, and safety, and insure that there is no deterioration or wear of the full and half-cock notches of the hammer, stretching of the sear spring, or wear of its lug. The mainspring leafs should not be broken.

57. When inspecting the handgrips with screw, insure that there are no cracks or splits, that the threads on the screw are intact, that the cutouts and grooves are not dirty, and that there is no dirt in the metal boss for the screw.

58. When inspecting the slide stop, insure that it is in good repair. The slide stop should not be bent or cracked. Insure that there is no chipping of the metal on the slide stop release.

59. When inspecting the magazine, pay special attention to the condition of the follower catch and the lug for the magazine catch; insure that the upper edges of the magazine body are not distorted (this deficiency leads to frequent stoppages during firing).

Inspection of the accessories (cleaning rod)

60. When inspecting the accessories, insure that the cleaning rod is not bent, dented, or scratched. The metal of the screwdriver tip should be intact.

Inspection of service ammunition

61. Inspect service ammunition to detect deficiencies that could lead to stoppages during firing.

Inspect cartridges before firing, during preparation for duty, and on special instruction.

62. When inspecting cartridges, it is important to determine:

— if there is corrosion or green deposits on the cases, especially around the primer. Are there dents or scratches on the cartridge that would prevent it from being chambered? Can the projectile be removed from the case by hand? Does the primer protrude above the base of the case? Cartridges with these defects should be selected out and turned in;

— if there are training cartridges among the service cartridges.

Ammunition that is dusty or dirty should be cleaned with a dry, clean cloth.

63. Ammunition should be stored in a dry place, and to the degree possible should be protected from the sun. During handling, do not subject it to damage. Protect it from dropping, moisture, dirt, and so on.

Preparation of the pistol for firing

64. Preparation of the pistol for firing is conducted to insure the continuous functioning of the pistol during firing and to preserve its normal zero. The following steps are required:

— inspect the pistol in disassembled form in accordance with paragraphs 52—59;

— inspect the pistol in assembled form in accordance with paragraph 51;

— inspect the ammunition as instructed in paragraphs 61 and 62;

— load the magazine with cartridges as instructed in paragraph 98;

— clean the bore and swab it dry immediately before firing.

Maintenance and storage of the pistol

65. The pistol should always be in serviceable condition. The service member to whom the weapon is issued is responsible to store the pistol, the holster, and accessories properly, and handle the pistol carefully and inspect it daily.

66. In the barracks or field lager environment, pistols are stored unloaded and out of the holsters in shelves or boxes with "cubby holes" in accordance with the Internal Service Regulations.

Storage of loaded pistols is permitted with special permission of the unit commander.

67. A service member may retain and store the pistol on his person during brief presences in populated areas.

68. During field exercises, on the march, during movement by rail or on vehicles, the pistol is carried in the holster on the belt, which should be securely fastened and correctly adjusted so that the holster does not strike any hard objects.

69. To prevent bulging or rupturing of the barrel during firing, **plugging or covering of the barrel by any means is prohibited.**

To avoid disruption of normal functioning of the pistol, it is prohibited to file down any of the components of the trigger mechanism.

70. In all situations not associated with firing, the thumb safety should be in the "safe" position. When placing the safety in the "fire" or "safe" position, the thumb safety should be manipulated to the extreme up or extreme down position.

71. If it becomes necessary to place the pistol in a damp holster, remove the pistol from the holster at the first opportunity, dry, clean, and lubricate the pistol, and dry the holster.

72. In hot, dusty regions, and also in coastal locales with high humidity, store the pistol in accordance with special instructions.

73. Decontamination of the pistol after contamination by persistent chemical agents should be conducted in accordance with special instructions of the chemical service unit.

Chapter 7

CONFIRMING THE PISTOL'S ZERO AND ESTABLISHING ITS NORMAL ZERO

General situation

74. A normal zero should be established for all pistols.

75. Confirmation of a pistol's zero is conducted:

— upon receipt of the pistol in the unit;

— after repair or replacement of any of the pistol's components that can influence the zero;

— upon detection during firing of abnormal target strikes.

76. In a combat situation, each commander should take every opportunity for periodic confirmation of his pistols' zeros.

Establishment and confirmation of the normal zero of a pistol

77. The confirmation of a pistol's zero is done by officers or excellent firers in the presence of the service members to whom the weapons are assigned. The senior supervisors, up to and including the unit commander, are required to insure the precise observation of the rules for confirmation of the pistols' zeros and for establishing their normal zero.

78. Before confirmation of the zero, the pistols are carefully inspected and detected deficiencies are corrected. An armorer with the necessary tools should be present during the inspection.

79. Confirmation of the zero is conducted in good conditions: in clear weather on a calm day or on an indoor range, or on a section of an outdoor range sheltered from the wind.

80. Confirmation of a pistol's zero is conducted by firing at 25 meters with ammunition from a single lot.

Firing is conducted at a black 25-cm diameter circle secured to a target 1 meter high and .5 meters wide.

81. The aimpoint is the bottom center edge of the black circle or the center of the circle. The aimpoint should be positioned at the firer's eye level.

Along a perpendicular line above the aimpoint is marked (with chalk or a colored pencil) the normal position of the mean point of impact, which should be 12.5 cm above the point of aim or coincide with the point of aim if the center of the circle is used. The marked point is the control point.

82. Confirmation of the pistol's zero is conducted from the standing unsupported or supported position (the ground, a bag filled with wood shavings), placed on any available object or support.

When firing from a support, the hand with the pistol should be balanced and not touching the support.

83. For confirmation of the pistol's zero, the firer fires four carefully aimed single shots.

84. Upon completion of firing, the target is examined to determine the shot group accuracy and the location of the mean point of impact.

85. The accuracy of the pistol's zero is considered normal if all four holes (in unusual circumstances, three if one of the holes sharply deviates from the remaining) fall within a circle (pattern) with a diameter of 15 centimeters (5.9 inches).

86. For a satisfactory accuracy of zero, the commander determines the mean point of impact and measures the magnitude of its deviation from the control point with the help of a centimeter ruler. For ease in measuring, two lines—vertical and horizontal—are drawn across the control point (with chalk or a colored pencil).

87. To determine the mean point of impact of four round strikes, connect any two round holes with a straight line and divide the distance between them in half. Join the point thus determined to a third hole with a straight line and divide this line into three equal parts. Join the tick mark nearest the first two holes with the fourth hole by a straight line, divided into four equal parts. The point at the third tick mark away from the fourth hole is the mean point of impact (figure 48).

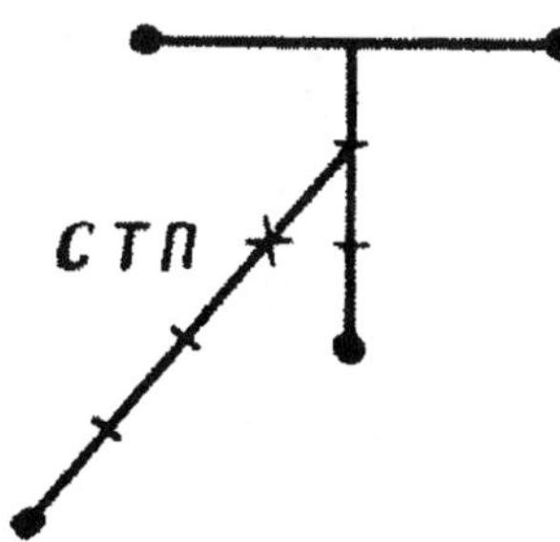

Figure 48. Determination of the mean point of impact of four holes

With a symmetrical placement of the holes, the mean point of impact can be determined by the following method: join the holes closest to each other with straight lines, then connect these two lines at their midpoints with a third straight line and divide this line in two equal parts; the midpoint of this line will be the mean point of impact (figure 49).

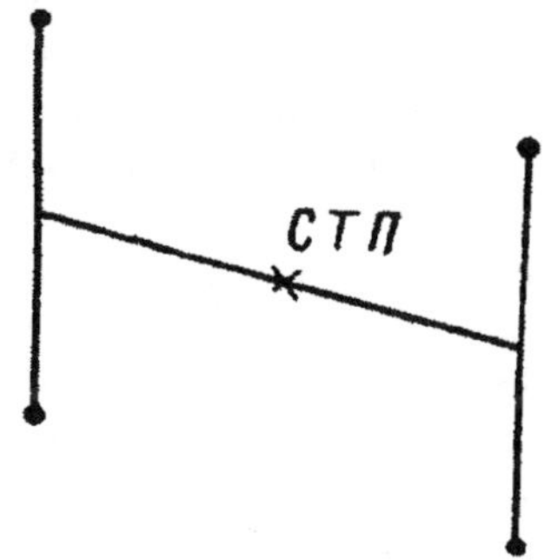

Figure 49. Determination of the mean point of impact of four symmetrically positioned holes.

To determine the mean point of impact of three holes, connect two holes with a straight line. Join the midpoint of this line with the third hole, and divide this line into three equal parts. The tick mark nearest the first line will be the mean point of impact (figure 50).

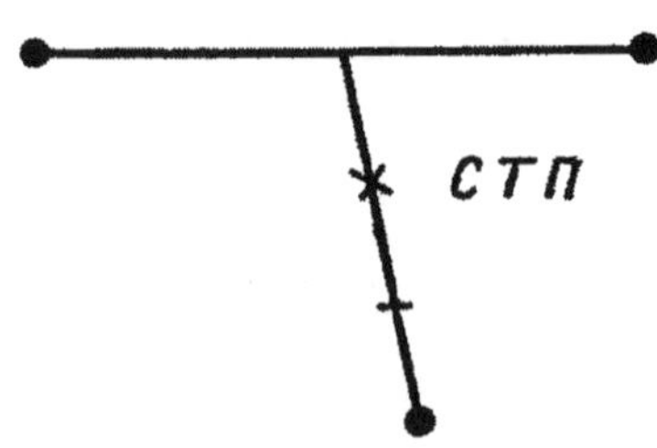

Figure 50. Determination of the mean point of impact of three holes.

88. Having determined the mean point of impact, the commander measures the magnitude of its deviation from the vertical and horizontal line. The mean point of impact should not deviate more than 5 centimeters from the control point in any direction. If the mean point of impact deviates from the control point by more than 5 centimeters, then the pistol must be turned in to the repair facility or armorer for appropriate adjustment or replacement of the rear sight. The rear sight is replaced with a lower (higher) sight if the mean point of impact is higher (lower) than the control point. The rear sight is moved to the left (right) if the mean point of impact is to the right (left) of the control point.

Note. Filing down of the front sight is prohibited.

89. Confirmation of the pistol's zero is considered complete when the pistol meets the requirements for a normal zero regarding both accuracy and location of mean point of impact.

90. Upon completion of confirmation of the pistol's zero, the rear sight is staked with a punch; the old mark on the rear sight is removed and a new mark is struck in its place.

Note. Removal of marks on the side of the slide is prohibited.

91. The results and time of confirmation of the pistol's zero are recorded in the report log. The round strikes are recorded as points or dots, and the mean point of impact as a cross.

Deficiencies that disrupt the pistol's normal zero

92. The following common deficiencies are causes of abnormal pistol zeros:

— the front sight blade is bent or dented, causing displacement of the bullets in the direction opposite the displacement of the upper portion of the blade;

— the rear sight has been moved, causing displacement of the bullets in the direction of the sight's movement;

— nicks at the muzzle of the barrel, causing displacement of the bullets to the side opposite the dents;

— erosion of the bore (especially at the muzzle), deterioration (rounding) of the lands, chipping and nicks in the bore, loosening of the rear sight—all increase the dispersion of bullets.

PART TWO

METHODS AND CONDUCT OF FIRE WITH THE PISTOL

Chapter 8

METHODS OF FIRING THE PISTOL

General situation

93. The pistol is fired from the standing, kneeling, prone positions, supported and unsupported, seated on a horse, in a vehicle or wagon, and so on. The firer can execute all firing methods quickly without losing sight of the target.

94. Firing the pistol combines the following tasks:

— **preparation for firing** (charging the pistol and assuming a firing position);

— **conduct of firing** (aiming, squeezing the trigger);

— **cessation of firing** (cessation of trigger action, manipulating the thumb safety to the "safe" position, unloading the pistol.

95. In combat, the pistol is fired independently [at the will of the firer].

96. For training purposes, commands are given for firing from various positions. For example, **"From the prone position** (from the kneeling or standing position), **at the deserter,—fire!"** On this command, take up the designated position, take the weapon off "safe" (push the thumb safety down) and, aiming, fire a double action shot. Firing on this command can also be conducted by first cocking the hammer. In this case, after the hammer is cocked, the firer need only aim and squeeze the trigger.

97. To execute the firing methods that will ensure the most accuracy and convenient actions of the firer, each service member should select the most comfortable and stable firing position in accordance with his individual preferences, keeping a uniform position of the pistol in the hand and the most comfortable position of the body, hands, and legs.

Preparation for firing

98. When preparing for firing, on the command "Load" the firer should:

— remove the pistol from the holster; remove the magazine from the handgrip; place the pistol back into the holster;

— load the magazine with cartridges as follows: hold the magazine in the left hand (figure 51). With the right hand, insert the cartridges into the magazine one behind the other, pushing down on the cartridges with the right thumb. After the cartridge passes the upper curved edges of the magazine body's side walls, move it to the rear so that the primer is up against the magazine's rear wall.

Figure 51. *Loading cartridges into the magazine.*

— remove the pistol from the holster with the right hand and insert the magazine into the handgrip;

— deliver a cartridge into the chamber as follows: take the weapon off "safe" (push the thumb safety down). With the left hand, pull the slide to the rear and release it.

— place the weapon on "safe" (with the right thumb, push up on the safety so that the red dot is covered). Place the pistol in the holster.

Note. In a combat situation, the pistol should be loaded ahead of time.

99. To assume a standing firing position (figure 52), it is necessary to:

— rotate one-half turn to the left and, without leaning on the right foot, extend it forward about one shoulder width (as suitable according to height) toward the target, distributing the body's weight equally on both legs;

— unfasten the flap and remove the pistol from the holster;

— hold the pistol perpendicular with the muzzle upward even with the right eye, maintaining the position of the right hand at chin level. The left hand should hang freely along the body or be placed behind the back;

— holding the pistol with the muzzle upward, place the thumb of the right hand on the safety and push it downward (take the weapon off "safe"). Place the index finger in the trigger guard, not touching the trigger.

Notes: 1. If firing left handed, the body position is reversed: remove the pistol from the holster with the right hand and transfer it to the left hand.

2. When firing with a preliminary cocking of the hammer, and

Figure 52. *The standing firing position.*

not double action, after taking the pistol off "safe", draw the hammer back to full cock with the right thumb.

100. To assume a kneeling firing position (figure 53) place the left foot to the rear so that the toes of the left foot are aligned with the heel of the right foot. Quickly drop to the left knee and sit back on the heel. Hold the right lower leg as perpendicular as possible, the toes pointed in the direction of the target. Remove the pistol from the holster, take it off "safe" (push the safety down), cock the hammer for single-action firing, and hold the pistol as instructed in paragraph 99.

Figure 53. The kneeling firing position

101. To assume a prone firing position (figure 54), rotate one-half turn to the right and simultaneously extend the right leg forward a half step. Quickly drop to the left knee, then, leaning on the ground with the left arm in the direction of the target, stretch out to the prone position with toes pointed outward. Remove the pistol from the holster, take it off "safe" and cock the hammer as instructed in paragraph 99 if firing is to be conducted single action. After taking the weapon off "safe", place the index finger of the right hand in the trigger guard, not touching the trigger.

Firing a shot

102. To shoot from all positions, one must select an aim point. Maintaining observation of the target, hold the pistol by the handgrip. Extend the right hand with the pistol forward.

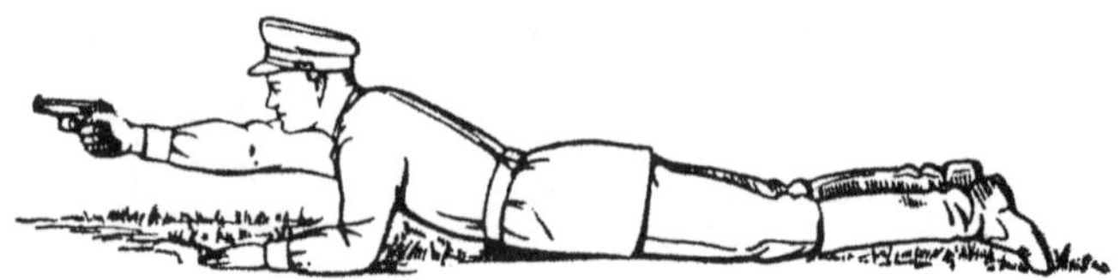

Figure 54. The prone firing position.

Place the index finger of this hand on the trigger up to the first joint. Extend the right thumb along the left side of the handgrip parallel to the barrel (figure 55). Hold the extended right hand loosely, without tenseness. Hold this hand on a plane that passes through the axis of the bore and the elbow (figure 56). Do not press on the handgrip of the pistol and, to the degree possible, grip it in a uniform manner.

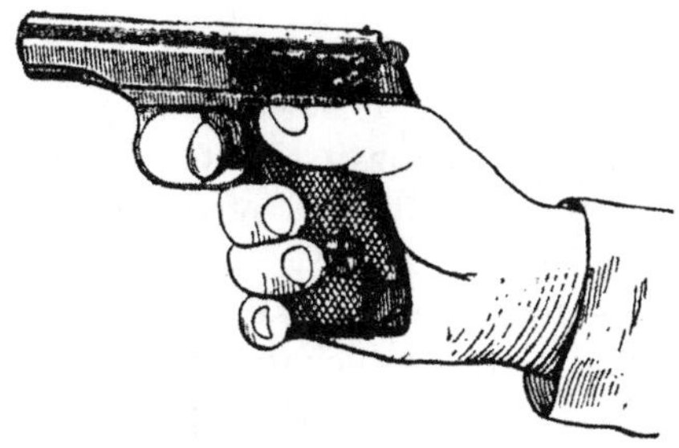

***Figure* 55.** *How to hold the pistol during firing.*

***Figure* 56.** *Firing from the standing position.*

103. For aiming, exhale, then momentarily hold the breath, and close the left eye. With the right eye, center the front sight blade in the rear sight notch with its top level with the top of the rear sight. In this position, move the pistol to the aim point (without lowering it) and simultaneously begin putting pressure on the trigger.

Note. If it is difficult for the firer to close the left eye, he can aim with both eyes open.

104. To squeeze the trigger it is necessary, while holding one's breath, to press smoothly with the first joint of the index finger on the trigger. The hammer, unnoticed by the firer, is released from full cock, rotates forward, and the pistol fires.

If the hammer has already been cocked, the trigger will have some free movement (slack), during which the shot will not be fired.

When squeezing the trigger, the finger is drawn straight to the rear. The firer should smoothly increase pressure on the trigger while maintaining the front sight blade on the aim point. When the front sight deviates from the aim point, the firer, neither increasing nor decreasing the pressure on the trigger, should correct the lay and, as soon as the front sight again coincides with the aim point, again increase the pressure on the trigger. When the hammer drops there should be no significant displacement of the front sight from the target. The effort to fire exactly at the moment when the front sight coincides with the aim point can in itself cause jerking, resulting in an imprecise shot. If the firer, squeezing the trigger, feels that he cannot hold his breath any longer, he must without increasing or decreasing the trigger squeeze take a breath and, again holding it, continue to squeeze the trigger smoothly.

Ceasing fire

105. A cease-fire can be **temporary** or **complete**.

For a temporary cessation of firing, the command "Cease Fire" is issued. On this command, the firer should stop squeezing the trigger. Holding the pistol in the right hand, with the thumb raise the safety up so that it covers the red dot (put the weapon on "safe"), and, if necessary, unload the pistol.

To reload the pistol:

— remove the magazine from the handgrip;

— place a loaded magazine in the handgrip;

— if firing is anticipated, take the weapon off "safe" (push the thumb safety down) and, if firing will be conducted with the hammer cocked [single action], cock the hammer. (If all cartridges were expended before reloading, it is necessary to pull the slide to the rear and release it.)

For a complete ceasefire, the command **"Unload"** is given. On this command, the firer should:

— stop squeezing the trigger;

— put the weapon on "safe";

— unload the pistol;

To unload the pistol:

— remove the magazine from the handgrip;

— put the weapon off "safe" (push the thumb safety down);

— remove the cartridge from the chamber by holding the pistol in the right hand by the handgrip, placing the left thumb and index finger on the slide grips, pulling the slide rearward and releasing it. Pick up the cartridge ejected from the chamber from the ground (floor), and clean it with a cloth;

— put the weapon on "safe";

— place the pistol in the holster;

— remove the cartridges from the magazine: holding the magazine in the left hand, with the right thumb slide the cartridges one after the other forward on the magazine follower and catch them in the palm of the same hand (figure 57);

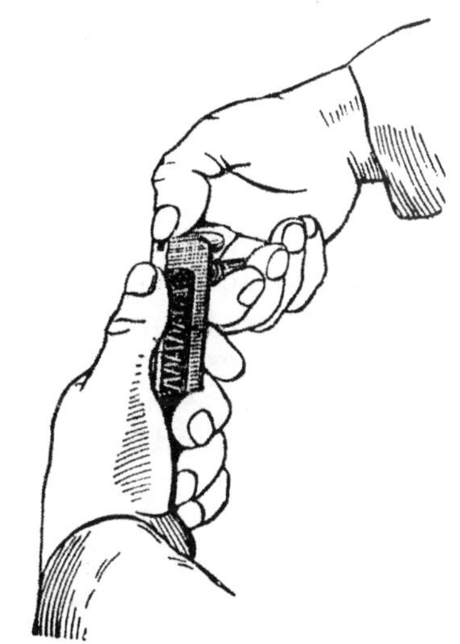

Figure 57. *Removal of the cartridges from the magazine.*

— remove the pistol from the holster; insert the magazine in the handgrip; again place the pistol in the holster and fasten the holster flap.

Firing with a support and from behind cover

106. A support is used to increase the effectiveness of fire. Depending on the height of the support, the firer should assume the appropriate firing position.

107. When firing with a support place the right hand with the pistol on the support so that the hand is suspended, and the pistol handgrip does not touch the support (figure 58).

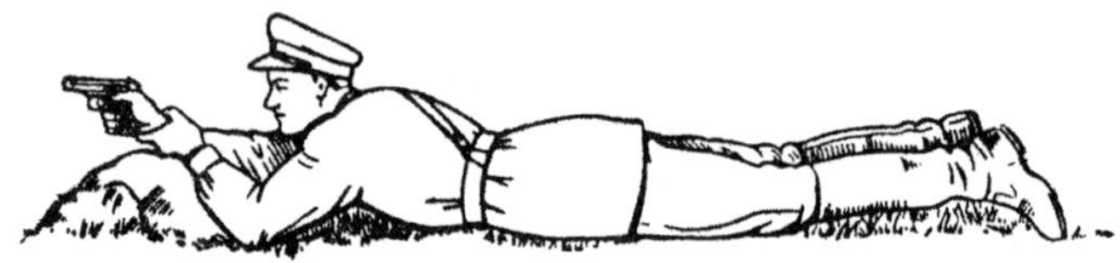

Figure 58. Prone supported firing position.

108. Cover is used to make the enemy's observation more difficult and for defense against his fire.

109. When firing off hand from behind cover, assume the appropriate position (standing, kneeling, prone) and place the right hand against a support so that the hand with the pistol is free (figures 59 and 60).

Firing from horseback

110. When firing from horseback, it is necessary to sit deeper in the saddle and, firmly gripping with the legs, assume the appropriate firing position in relationship to the target location.

When firing forward, extend the right hand with the pistol as far forward as possible over the horse's head, shorten the rein, put weight on the stirrups, and lean the body forward.

If the target is positioned low or quite near, and it is impossible to take aim over the horse's head, extend the hand with the

Figure 59. *Standing firing position from cover.*

Figure 60. *Kneeling firing position from cover.*

pistol to the right (left) in front of the horse's head. Rest the left hand with rein against the horse's withers.

For firing to the rear, hold a short rein with the left hand in the horse's withers, turn the body sharply to the right.

For firing to the right or left from the direction of travel, incline the body in the direction of the target, leaving the hand with rein on the horse's withers.

In all cases of firing from the horse, after turning or leaning the body, quickly extend the right hand with pistol in the direction of the target and fire the shot.

For firing at quick pace, aim along the upper portion of the slide and fire quick shots using double action.

Chapter 9

CONDUCT OF FIRE WITH THE PISTOL

General situation

111. Service personnel armed with the pistol conduct fire in combat at their own discretion, depending on the situation.

112. Fire from the pistol is characterized by the following data:

Trajectory versus line of sight in centimeters firing pistol zeroed normally at 25 meters

Distance (meters)	*maximum height of trajectory at given range*	*displacement of point of impact at given range*
10	+ 5.0	+0.5
15	+7.8	+0.3
20	+10.2	+0.2
25	+12.5	0
30	+13.9	-0.5
40	+16.0	-2.5
50	+16.8	-5.7

Radius of dispersion in centimeters

100% of bullets	*50% of bullets*
3.5	2.0
5.0	3.0
6.5	4.0
7.5	4.5
9.0	6.0
12.0	7.0
16.0	8.0

Note. For the third column, the plus (+) sign indicates displacement of mean point of impact above aimpoint, and the minus (-) sign indicates displacement of mean point of impact below aimpoint.

Selection of site for firing

113. The pistol is fired from any location and using any position that will insure the destruction of the target in the shortest possible time.

114. In combat, the firer himself selects the position for firing the pistol. He must consider the situation and the nature of the terrain in selecting a firing location.

115. The selected firing position should provide for the greatest ease of action, the most effective fire, and cover from enemy fire.

Target selection

116. Single enemy soldiers and officers out in the open who suddenly appear or are moving are targets for this pistol in combat.

117. The significance of the target should guide the selection of the target, with preference given to the closest and most vulnerable targets.

Selection of aimpoint

118. For the most reliable destruction of the target, consider the range to it and the magnitude of the trajectory/line of sight differential, using the table provided.

119. When firing at a stationary target at ranges up to 50 meters, select the aimpoint in each case in accordance with the target's position and height.

120. Conduct fire at targets moving directly toward your fire the same as at stationary targets.

To defeat targets moving at an angle to the plane of fire, shift the aimpoint along the target movement axis, taking into consideration the speed of its movement.

121. Conduct fire at targets that appear for a brief time or suddenly with double action, and take quick shots when the target is at the most favorable position.

Firing in limited visibility conditions

122. When firing at night during artificial illumination, great skill is demanded of the firer to be able to fire quickly.

During illumination of the target, the firer should quickly find the target and take a quick shot or fire a series of shots, depending on the duration of the illumination.

Firing at dusk (dawn) and under moonlight is conducted by the same principles as during the day.

123. At night, when it is impossible to illuminate the target and aim, fire snap shots at silhouettes or toward muzzle flashes and various sounds coming from the enemy's location.

Firing in conditions of chemical and radioactive contamination

124. Firing in conditions of chemical and radioactive contamination is done while wearing individual protective garments.

The principles of firing at various targets are the same as firing under normal conditions.

Supply and expenditure of ammunition in combat

125. Ammunition for the pistol is carried in the spare magazine in the holster. Each service member armed with the pistol is required to monitor his ammunition supply and expend it economically in battle.

Appendix A

CHARACTERISTICS OF THE 9-MM MAKAROV PISTOL (PM)

Weight of pistol with magazine, unloaded	730 grams / 25.7 ounces
Weight of pistol with magazine, eight cartridges	810 grams / 28.5 ounces
Length of pistol	161 mm / 6.3 inches
Height of pistol	126.75 mm / 5.0 inches
Barrel length	93 mm / 3.66 inches
Caliber	9mm [9 x 18]
Number of lands	4
Magazine capacity	8 rounds
Cartridge weight	10 grams
Projectile weight	6.1 grams / 94.1 grains
Cartridge length	25 mm / .98 inches
Combat rate of fire	30 shots per minute
Muzzle velocity	315 meters per second *1033 feet per second*

Appendix B

FIREARMS SAFETY

The 9mm Makarov Pistol is a firearm and a dangerous weapon. It is potentially lethal.

WARNING: If the 9mm Makarov Pistol, or any firearm, is carelessly or improperly handled, unintentional discharge could result and could cause injury, death, or damage to property.

Users of 9mm Makarov Pistols are advised to carefully read the instruction manual if one came with the firearm, prior to loading and firing. Your safety and the safety of others, including members of your family, depends on your understanding and mature compliance with the applicable instruction manual and your constant use of safe firearms handling practices. If you are unfamiliar with firearms, seek further advice through safe handling courses offered by local gun clubs, National Rifle Association approved instructors, or similar qualified organizations.

Russian Military Translations and Enterprise Desktop Publishing shall not be responsible for injury, death, or damage to property resulting from either intentional or unintentional discharge of a Makarov pistol.

Six Basic Firearms Safety Rules

1. Never put a round in the chamber until you are ready to shoot.
2. Always point the gun in a safe direction.
3. Keep the selector on safe until you are ready to fire.
4. Unload the weapon completely immediately after use, and double check the chamber.
5. Always ensure a gun is not loaded before cleaning or disassembling it.
6. Practice handling the gun empty before attempting to load and fire it.

WARNING: When you squeeze the trigger of any firearm, you must expect the firearm to fire, and you must take full responsibility for firing it. Your careful handling can avoid accidental discharge, and you can avoid accidental injury and death.

WARNING: This firearm may accidentally fire when a round is loaded into the chamber, if the firearm is dropped, or receives a blow to the muzzle or front of the gun. This can occur regardless of the hammer or safety positions. Extra care and strict use of safe handling procedures by the firearm user is mandatory and essential to minimize risk of accidents.

Firearm Safe Handling Rules

- Always handle your firearm as if it were loaded, so that you never fire it accidentally when you think it is unloaded.
- Never point your firearm at anything you do not want to shoot, so that if it fires accidentally, you will prevent injury, death, or damage to property.
- Never take anyone's word that a firearm is unloaded. Check for yourself with your fingers off the trigger and the gun pointed in a safe direction, so that you never fire the firearm accidentally when you think it is unloaded.
- Always make sure your firearm is not loaded and the slide or bolt is latched open before laying it down, or handing it to another person, so that it cannot be fired accidentally or when it is unsafe to fire it.
- Always keep and carry your firearm empty, with the hammer forward except when you intend to shoot, so that your firearm cannot be fired when you do not mean to fire it.
- Always be aware of possible risk from dropping your firearm. Some parts of the mechanism could be damaged. You may not see the damage, but if it is severe, the firearm may discharge and cause injury, death, or damage to property. If your firearm has been dropped, have it examined by a competent gunsmith before using it again.
- Never leave a firearm cocked ready to fire. This condition is extremely dangerous, and the firearm could easily be accidentally discharged, causing injury, death, or damage to property.
- Never leave a loaded firearm unattended. Someone, especially a child, may fire it and cause injury, death, or damage to property.

Firearm Safe Handling Rules

- Store your firearms and ammunition securely locked and in separate locations out of reach and sight of children. Children are naturally curious and do not always recognize or believe the real danger of guns.
- Always instruct children and others in your home to respect firearms. If you teach your children to shoot, teach them or get them trained by a qualified instructor to treat and use the firearm properly. Always supervise them closely. Always stress safety so that your children will not fire the firearm when it is unsafe to do so.
- Always be sure your shooting backstop is adequate to stop and contain bullets before beginning target practice, so that you do not hit anything outside the range shooting area.
- Always put a knowledgeable and responsible adult in charge to maintain safety control when a group is firing on a range. Obey his or her commands to maintain discipline and reduce the possibility of accidents.
- Always carry your firearm empty with the bolt latched open or slide locked open while on a range until preparing to fire. Keep it pointing toward the backstop when loading, firing, and unloading, to eliminate the risk of injury, death, or damage to property from premature or accidental discharge.
- Always be sure the barrel, bore, chamber, and action are clean and clear of obstructions. Clean a wet or fouled firearm immediately so that it will function correctly and safely.
- Always use only clean, dry, original, high quality, commercially manufactured ammunition in good condition that is appropriate to the caliber of your firearm. Gun and ammunition manufacturers design their products within exacting engineering safety limits. Handloads and remanufactured ammunition are sometimes outside of those limits and can be so unsafe as to explode in the chamber and receiver to cause injury, death, or damage to property. The use of remanufactured or hand loaded ammunition is not recommended.
- Always check that ammunition is clean and undamaged. Do not force ammunition into the chamber. Forcing dam-

aged ammunition into the chamber could damage your firearm and could result in injury, death, or damage to property.

• Never drink alcoholic beverages or take drugs before or during shooting, as your vision and judgment could be seriously impaired, making your gun handling unsafe.

• Always seek a doctor's advice if you are taking medication, to be sure that neither your condition nor your medication render you unfit to shoot and handle your firearm safely.

Firearm Safe Handling Rules

• Always wear and encourage others to wear ear protection when shooting, especially on a range. Without ear protection, the noise from your firearm and other guns close to you could leave a "ringing" in the ears for some time after firing. Temporary and permanent hearing loss can result from unprotected exposure to noise from firearms.

• Always wear and encourage others to wear protective shooting glasses. Flying particles could damage your eyes and cause blindness. Protective glasses designed for shooting should prevent such injury. Ensure protective glasses are designed for protection while shooting firearms.

• Always keep the safety selector switch set to "safe" when the firearm is loaded and cocked, until you are aiming at your target and intend to fire. This will reduce the risk of accidental firing.

• If your firearm fails to fire when you pull the trigger, hold it, keeping it pointed toward the target, and wait 30 seconds. If a hangfire (slow ignition) has occurred, the round should fire within 30 seconds. If the round does not fire within 30 seconds, remove the magazine, eject the round and examine the primer. If the firing pin indent on the primer is light, misaligned, or non-existent, have a competent gunsmith examine your firearm. If the firing pin indent on the primer appears normal in comparison with previously fired rounds, assume faulty ammunition. Segregate misfired rounds from other live ammunition and empty cases. Reload and continue firing. Dispose of misfired rounds in accordance with the ammunition manufacturer's instructions.

- Never use your firearm if it fails to operate properly. Never force a jammed round, as a round may explode causing serious injury, possible death, or severe damage to your firearm.
- Always keep clear and keep others clear of the cartridge ejection port. Spent cartridges are ejected with enough force to cause injury, and the ejection port must be clear to ensure safe ejection of spent cartridges or live rounds. Never place your fingers in the ejection area. You could be burned by hot metal or injured by the bolt or slide moving forward.
- Never put your finger inside the trigger guard or squeeze the trigger until you are aiming at a target and are ready to shoot. This will prevent you from firing the firearm when it is pointing in an unsafe direction.
- Always be absolutely sure of your target, and the area around and behind it, before you squeeze the trigger. A bullet could travel miles beyond your target. If in doubt, don't shoot.
- Never attempt to fire with water in the barrel. Water can accumulate if your firearm is exposed to heavy rain or fog. Open the bolt or slide and allow the water to drain. Clean and dry the weapon before firing, if possible.

Firearm Safe Handling Rules

- Never shoot at a hard surface such as a rock, or a liquid surface such as water. A bullet may ricochet and travel in any direction to strike you, or an object you cannot see, causing injury, death, or damage to property.

- Never fire your firearm near an animal unless the animal is trained to accept the noise. An animal's startled reaction could injure it or cause an accident.

- Never indulge in "horseplay" while holding your firearm, or with anyone else holding a firearm, as it may be accidentally discharged.

- Never walk, climb, or follow a companion with your firearm cocked ready to fire. To eliminate the risk of accidental discharge, hold your firearm so that you can always control the direction of the muzzle, and keep the safety selector lever set to "safe."
- Always make sure your firearm is not loaded before cleaning or storing it, so that it cannot be fired when it is unsafe to do so.
- When disassembling or assembling a firearm, wear safety glasses in case you lose control of a spring or spring-loaded component that could injure your eyes.
- Never abuse your firearm by using it for any purpose other than shooting.
- Never dry fire the firearm when the receiver is open, and do not alter parts, as the level of safety could be reduced.